THERE WAS ONCE A TIME

THERE WAS ONCE A TIME
Anne-Marie Rasmussen

HARCOURT BRACE JOVANOVICH
NEW YORK AND LONDON

Library of Congress Cataloging in Publication Data

Rasmussen, Anne-Marie.
There was once a time.

1. Rasmussen, Anne-Marie.   2. Rockefeller family.
I. Title.
CT275.R266A33   332'.092'4 [B]   74-20803
ISBN 0-15-189481-7

BCDE

This book is dedicated with love to
Steven, Jr., Ingrid, and Jennifer Rockefeller

Acknowledgment

I wish to acknowledge the assistance of Betty W. Sapoch in the writing of this book.

Contents

Illustrations

Foreword

This book is not intended to be the story of a "poor little rich girl." I have had unique experiences, and I have been asked many questions regarding my life as Mrs. Steven Clark Rockefeller. I hope the following account will answer some of these questions for others as well as for myself.

There are a few personal things that have been omitted, but the story—subjective, of course, seen entirely through my eyes—is as nearly complete as I can make it.

A doctor friend recently told me, "Mia, you have to say good-bye to your past before you can say hello to a future." Forgetting about being married to a man I loved who was born a Rockefeller is a difficult task, especially with three children who are a part of both of us and bear a name that has powerful associations not just in this country but throughout the world. I may never be able to say good-bye completely, but by putting my story in writing I am trying to let go of my illusions.

ISLANDS

• 1 •

Borøya

Almost everyone has his own idea of what it would be like to live on an island. Movies do much to romanticize languid, lush islands in tropical waters, and the Swiss Family Robinson made life on their desert island seem enchanted. The theme of island adventures has a strong appeal for many Americans. Even the Rockefellers, though they cannot exactly be called a typical family, were imbued with the notion that islands are something special. An island, for them, was a refuge from their particular pressures. In visiting their various sanctuaries they sought a communion with nature that would sanctify their daily life, bring them peace, provide them with an escape from the sins of the fathers.

I can still remember being incredulous when I heard that Mrs. David Rockefeller was "collecting" many of the islands off the coast of Maine. She had advisers and scouts who did nothing but seek available islands for her to buy before they were "all gone." Steven himself purchased one called Hat Island, and that remote piece of land excited and comforted him more than all of Rockefeller Center ever could. He loved "getting down to basics" there. I firmly believe that Michael, Steven's younger brother, lost his life in a similar kind of search—a search for something basic, natural, and primitive. The whole family seemed, to me, to be periodically in flight; all of them needed to leave the publicity-haunted mainland now and then, and seek solace on some island. There was one in the Caribbean that even I fell in love with. Mr. Laurance Rockefeller took a romantic island in the sun, St. John, and built Caneel Bay Plantation there—a place fit for less rugged types, like me, who wanted to get away from everything except comfort.

Sometimes I was convinced that the Rockefellers were being overly diplomatic and solicitous when, at various family gatherings, they asked me to tell them about the island off the southern coast of Norway on which I was born and brought up. They had so many important topics and so many fascinating people to discuss that I couldn't really believe they were curious about my tiny homeland or interested in my simple stories about islanders.

I told them that to me "island" only brought back memories of loneliness—that on Borøya I was always aware of being far away from the rest of the world, and believed I was missing something marvelous that surely must be going on "out there." I wondered why anyone who lived on the mainland, much less owned huge tracts of it, would ever want to leave it for a rocky, windy, desolate piece of land entirely surrounded by water.

I've tried often to look back on that insignificant bit of land in the North Sea, and to understand what, if anything, directed me along the path that led from the simple home of a grocer to a domestic job in the United States to marriage into one of the most prominent families in the world.

• • •

Borøya is a hilly island, rocky and wooded, with small open meadows here and there. From any of the hills you can look out toward other, smaller islands, and wherever you look there is the North Sea.

There were between twenty and thirty houses on Borøya when I was a child, all built of wood, with tile roofs, and they were occupied mainly by fishermen and their families. The men were good at fishing, and the women were good cooks, good housekeepers, good wives and mothers, in that order.

Our home was the first to be constructed on the island when settlers began moving out from the mainland in the nineteenth century. Part of the house itself had been brought from the mainland, and the rest had been built by my grandfather and his family. It was not more than two hundred yards from the harbor, and I can remember that on stormy nights the salt spray blew against the windows of the bedroom I shared with my sister.

Pappa lived in that house for sixty-eight years. He spent his youth fishing, and saving his money, hoping he could finally establish his own business on the island. It took him twenty years, but he did realize his dream, a *Landhandel,* or country store, situated right at the harborside. There he sold everything from groceries and dry goods to all the equipment needed by the fishermen. He also built a wharf and started a fish-export business from it. The other men on the island were pleased at that, preferring to deal with my father rather than with fish exporters from the mainland.

His *Landhandel* and his wharf kept him busy, but Pappa was active in every aspect of life on the island—even in local politics. He had always felt that in starting his own business he would be doing more than bettering life for himself and his family. He would gain a closer contact with all his friends and neighbors than he would have had as a fisherman, and that was part of his dream, too. He believed that he could help to make life better for everybody on

Borøya and the other islands. So for many years he was a member of the town council and the parish council (the church itself was on the mainland, but every other Sunday my grandfather came to the island to conduct services), and he also served as spokesman for the outlying islands. He really did become instrumental in the growth and development of the community.

All the islanders worked together, were concerned about one another, and involved themselves in one another's lives. Eventually they joined forces to build a schoolhouse, and under a wonderful teacher, Miss Ingeborg Birkeland, it became one of the best in the district of Søgne. So when I was a child the island was, in its own way, a thriving and busy place. But today it stands almost deserted. The original homesteaders have gone to the mainland to spend some years in comfort away from the sea, and the young have also made lives for themselves there. Well-to-do tourists from Oslo, rather like Norwegian versions of the Rockefellers, have bought up many of the homes, and Borøya, too, has become a sanctuary—for birds and for people in flight.

It was about the time the new schoolhouse was built that I was born. Kristian Rasmussen had one son by an earlier marriage; now, close to fifty, he finally became father of a girl. Even on an island in the North Sea, that was cause for celebration, and visitors streamed into our home to welcome the new baby. But two years later, when my sister was born, there was no time for festivities. That April, a month earlier, the Second World War had come to Norway, and almost everyone was preoccupied with wartime sacrifices.

Looking back, I can truly say that all the islanders lived in constant fear throughout the years of the war. Of course I was aware of their fear, and I have many vivid memories of that period, about which I'll say more later. But to a child wartime conditions were something to be taken for granted.

I was proud of my two years' head start on Torhild, and like all older sisters I must have boasted to her, and bossed her around a good deal, and teased her. But we did enjoy each other's company in that secluded place.

During the summers, Torhild learned to swim in the ocean. She enjoyed the cold, cold water, and so did most of the other children on Borøya, but I was quite afraid of it. Besides, Mamma was a wonderful swimmer. I couldn't imagine ever being able to swim as beautifully as she did, so why try? What I liked was a little playhouse that Uncle Johan, my mother's brother-in-law, built for me out of some scraps of wood. It stood right next to our house, and although it was barely large enough to hold two little girls at the same time, I loved it. When I played there I could show my mother that I, too, was a good housekeeper and organizer. It was also a place where I could go to get away from chores I didn't like, such as ironing, and where I could have privacy whenever I needed it.

We had other chores. My parents always kept between ten and fifteen sheep. Not all sheep are good mothers, and many years Torhild and I had full-time jobs feeding unwanted lambs from a baby's bottle until they were old enough to eat grass. That was my greatest interest, I think, though not Torhild's. It was always a real sorrow to both of us when we couldn't keep the lambs we had taken turns feeding—they had become real pets, and followed us around like dogs.

There have never been any cars or bicycles on Borøya, and when I was a child there weren't even any roads. Torhild and I walked to school along a stony path that had simply been made there over the years by the passing of many feet. On rainy or snowy days, I loved checking the footprints ahead of me, wondering who had walked there and what kinds of shoes they had worn, and it was fun to put my little foot in a big footprint made by a man.

I enjoyed school, and got to be on very friendly terms with the teacher. Miss Birkeland was in her fifties then, and I found excuses to visit her in the evening, in her own small house. I often did my homework there, and after I was through we used to talk together—long, serious conversations about life in general. I felt not like one of her students, but one of her best friends.

No other person I have known anywhere has influenced me as much. Years later, when Steven told me about his years at Deerfield Academy, I realized that Miss Birkeland had played the same role in my life that Dr. Frank Boyden, the headmaster of Deerfield, had played in his. She was a uniquely intelligent and stimulating human being, and she devoted herself to the children of Borøya for thirty-six years.

I remember Pappa as being strong, quiet, gentle, and exceptionally patient and understanding with his family and others. He would stand for hours in the store, pipe in mouth, dealing with everyone's problems, the local equivalent of a psychiatrist. The only thing he didn't attempt to change was the weather. *"Ja, ja,"* he'd say, "it will be better tomorrow." It's a wise man who knows his limits! He had a deep-rooted faith in God, and drew strength from it. With his weather-beaten face and hands, he was as much a part of that island as the rocks, the sand, the sea gulls, and the fish.

Mamma, on the other hand, was full of emotions and longings, and often deeply melancholy. She had come out to the island long ago on a visit, and then settled down as Pappa's housekeeper. He had been a widower for some time, and Sander, his son by his first marriage, was by then in his teens. Mamma got along well with Sander, and with Kristian Rasmussen, though he was nineteen years older than she was. But she wasn't particularly enthusiastic about the lonely island, and she worked for Pappa for three years before they decided to get married. Sander married when I was four, and moved to the mainland. I adored him, but he was so much older than I was that he seemed more like an uncle than a half brother.

Mamma was often very sad, and winter, with its meager ration of sunshine, seemed to depress her particularly. But she was musically gifted, and I spent many hours listening to the sentimental songs she played: on a parlor organ, a violin, a *munnspill,* or harmonica, a Norwegian harp called a *harpeleik*—and her favorite comb! She also had a clear and beautiful voice. Sometimes Torhild and I would cry at the songs she sang by heart, even the supposedly cheerful ones, because of something about the way she sounded and looked as she sang.

From my mother I learned to carry a tune. Often I would play on the *harpeleik* and Mamma would sing as neighbors and visitors gathered to sit in our beautiful garden and listen to us perform. (Mamma had the traditional green thumb, and that garden was a real local attraction. Every summer people came to admire her magnificent roses, which grew up against the unusual stone walls that she had built with her own hands.) In any event, she became convinced, to my horror, that I was destined to become a great musician or singer. She told me about a dream she'd had the day before I was born, in which she was a little girl again, sitting in a swing. She heard and was filled with wonder by beautiful singing and music. The message of the dream was always in her mind, and because of it I was sent to the mainland at the age of ten to take music lessons from the church organist. It was a forty-five-minute trip by boat, followed by a good half hour's walk to his home, and I quickly tired of the lessons with the old man. I announced that I would not go back because he had bad breath! I think now that I felt burdened by the expectations the famous dream aroused. And I never did fulfill them—though I went on playing the *harpeleik,* and much later I studied the guitar and learned to play well enough to accompany myself in some simple songs, just for my own enjoyment and for my children.

Often in those years on Borøya when I was alone, I would

take out Mamma's old love letters, which were folded very carefully and kept in a beautiful bag lined in white polka-dotted silk. My hands knew exactly where the bag was in Mamma's third drawer, beneath her underclothes, and also how to put it carefully back. It contained many beautiful and tender letters sent to her before she was married—but none of them were from Pappa. Those letters from other young men, all strangers to me, fitted very nicely in the dream world I was slowly constructing. I began to imagine a place "out there" filled with love and romance, with good smells, and with delicate things that looked and felt like the lining of Mamma's bag—a place where lively music and dancing were not a "sin," a place where it was never cold and damp, where you didn't have to bathe in the North Sea or clean fish in it, either. And I dreamed of men and boys who would be romantic and loving to me.

Summer was the time of year when I was least lonely. The days were full and seemed never to end. In Norway, in summer, there is hardly ever complete darkness or full night, but a twilight that seems magical and lasts for only a few hours. The evenings are balmy and rose colored, slightly unreal, just right for a sunshine-starved, dreamy, romantic Scandinavian girl.

Those days of the midnight sun brought lots of excitement, especially when the tourists discovered our remote island and began to trickle in. Torhild always chose to avoid the strangers, but seemed to be delighted by my courage in getting promptly acquainted with them. I took care of their children, I listened to their tales, and I watched in utter amazement and fascination as some families sunbathed and swam nude, often wondering if they didn't see me or didn't care. But if Torhild was aware of the nudists, she never acknowledged it. She stayed far away, and spent her time splashing, playing, and perfecting her swimming in the ocean.

So many good things happened in the summer that I hoped the happy memories would last all winter. They never did.

Autumn was the most changeable time of the year, and the beach reflected the turbulence of the sea. It was then that the most unusual shells and driftwood could be found on the ocean side of the island. The traffic on my father's wharf also became more lively. The fishing boats came and went more frequently as the men delivered the day's catch to my father, who sent it on to the city in the morning by ferry. The pace seemed to quicken, as if we were all trying to fend off the coming of winter.

But no one could forestall a Norwegian winter. It arrived too soon, and settled over us like an icy mantle, wrapping us in its gloom until the following spring.

When I was fourteen my Uncle Andres, my mother's oldest brother, came back from the United States for a visit. It was the first time that I had met him, but he looked at me and asked, "Where were you the last time I was here?" I didn't understand that he was joking. I thought he knew perfectly well that I hadn't been born the last time he was home, and wondered if he had been in "that country" too long. I noticed he had partly forgotten his mother tongue, and he mixed too much English with his Norwegian for my ears to keep up with him. He also kept his change in his pants pockets instead of a change purse, as we did. He didn't seem to tuck his shirt in any more, saying it was fashionable now to let the tails hang out—he called it the Truman look.

He was a mounted policeman in Manhattan, his beat was Harlem, and his world seemed full of excitement and danger. I begged him to take me back to New York City with him, promising verbally and on paper to be a good girl—no haircuts, no lipstick, no dancing, and, of course, no smoking. But not only did he feel that I had to grow up before I visited him; he also told me he was going to marry a friend of Mamma's he had met that summer.

I believed that my heart was broken, but when Uncle Andres left Norway and me that summer to go back to New York with Tante Margit, I found that I had a lot to hope for. I knew then that somehow, someday, I would get to America. I pictured New York City as a kind of fairyland where anything and everything could and would happen to me. I thought about the skyscrapers, and tried to imagine what Uncle Andres meant by "elevator." I especially wanted to go to Harlem—at night, because he had said it was a bad place to be at any time and was especially bad at night. For by now, in my world in Norway, whatever Mamma or other grownups called sin was turning out to be just what I wanted most to do.

Childhood days passed—forlornness, play, work—but not my dream. As we grew older, Torhild and I had to assume more responsibilities. Soon we began to help Pappa in the store. It was great fun at first, but lost its appeal when summer arrived and I wasn't able to spend all my time keeping up with the comings and goings of the tourists. I was still able to do some baby-sitting, though, and that helped my "send-Mia-to-America" fund. Sometimes I wondered if I would ever earn enough to pay my way on the big ship I had watched passing by our island, always wishing to be a sea gull so I could fly aboard.

As I grew into my teens I became more and more restless and difficult to handle. My moods became as changeable as the sea around me. The work, the seemingly dull life, and Torhild's growing contentment and quiet nature stifled me. I could no longer accept my place on this island where chance had so arbitrarily placed me. Knowing that I, with my growing frustration, couldn't be contained, my parents gave their consent for me to leave Norway. My savings were not quite sufficient, but Pappa helped out.

Borøya

I was just barely eighteen, with a one-way ticket to the United States, a few extra dollars, and a lot of anticipation and dreams. Nothing else seemed to matter at the time. I was on my way to the promised land.

• 2 •

Manhattan

I left Kristiansand S on August 23, 1956, aboard the
Oslofjord. To my surprise and dismay, I was booked into a
cabin with two ladies who were Norwegian-American
Fundamentalists. They read the Bible more than I wanted to
see or hear, and it made me feel guilty over what I thought I
was leaving behind. However, they were very motherly and
took great pride in their ability to protect me from, as well as
introduce me to, all the luxury and freedom of the high seas.
I still correspond with one of them, who goes on being
interested in what happens to me.

I was chagrined at being the only one to be seasick—and I
was worried, too. If living on the island and spending most
of my life in boats hadn't prepared me at least for the ocean
part of my pilgrimage, what would happen to me on "the
other side"?

Upon my arrival in New York Harbor, after nine days on

the Atlantic Ocean, I wrote to my parents: "Strange to have finally arrived in New York City. Sorry to have to spend my first night on a boat! Also, did you know that Manhattan is an *island*? Couldn't sleep one hour. I kept looking at the millions of lights and constant moving of cars. There was no stop to the traffic. Americans must not sleep very much."

Early the next morning everything and everybody seemed to change. The language became predominantly English, and the people seemed rushed and nervous as we prepared to meet the men from the immigration service. Fortunately, Uncle Andres came to pick me up wearing his policeman's uniform, and the customs officials on the pier sent me through the line like a diplomat. So my uncle and his America impressed me all over again.

We drove together to his home in the Bronx, but I stayed with my aunt and uncle only a few days before deciding to plunge right in and look for employment. I was determined to find a live-in job, which would not only take care of the housing and food problem, but give me an opportunity to become fluent in English.

I went to a Scandinavian employment agency on Madison Avenue, hoping someone there would understand my Norwegian complete with a heavy Sørlands dialect. The very first opening described to me was for a kitchen maid in the home of "an important family" on Fifth Avenue. My interviewer was so impressed with her client that I wondered why she didn't take the position herself. But it sounded like a fine challenge to me, and I promised to give it a good Nordic try. I proudly sent this flash home: "Now I am going to start to work for a well-known family. Their name is Rockenfellere. I am going to start to earn a few dollars instead of *kroner*. Wonder how that is going to feel? I will let you know shortly."

Accompanied by my aunt, who came along to help with the translating, and carrying my few belongings in the suitcase I had borrowed from Mamma, who was a traveler only in her daydreams, I approached an overpolite and well-dressed gentleman at the entrance to the Rockefeller's apartment. I thought he was very nice even to bother about me to the extent of calling Mrs. Rockefeller's secretary, Mrs. Bay, to let her know that I had arrived. Then this extremely formal man, who reminded me of a police officer in Norway, escorted me on the first elevator of my life—one dream come true!—under a sign marked SERVICE.

Mrs. Bay interviewed me for Mrs. Rockefeller, who would not be returning from Seal Harbor, in Maine, for a few more days. Understanding almost no English, I couldn't really tell how the interview was going. So I was surprised when my aunt told me that I was acceptable to Mrs. Bay, who liked my blue eyes and big smile. I thought these were strange recommendations for a maid's job!

I can remember, now, being impressed by how well groomed and meticulously made-up Mrs. Bay was: it was the first time I had ever seen anyone wearing complete make-up. If her secretary looked like this, I thought, what was Mrs. Rockefeller herself going to look like? So I was truly surprised when I first met Mrs. Rockefeller, who didn't appear to have on any make-up except lipstick. She greeted me warmly and welcomed me to their home—the first American I met who spoke slowly and clearly enough for me to understand.

Much later I met Mr. Nelson Rockefeller, who shook my hand firmly and said he hoped I would be happy and stay long in their home. At least that was how I interpreted his smile and his kind voice at the time. He seemed friendly, and I liked him immediately because he seemed to enjoy being alive.

The Rockefellers had a very considerable household staff, and when we all got together there were enough of us to hold a prayer meeting. The others, on the whole, were kind and helpful, and patient about my indoctrination. I was both thrilled and amused to be in the company of so many people from other European countries, and I was eager to begin my collection of English words so I would be able to communicate with everyone. My textbook and my greatest joy was the *Daily News*, which I began to study religiously. The New York *Times* was also passed on to the staff when the family had finished reading it, but I couldn't imagine how anyone had enough time in one day—or in a whole week, for that matter—to read it. I decided it must be a newspaper published exclusively for the wealthy, who had nothing else to do.

I hadn't been on the job more than a few days before I first set eyes on a photograph of Steven Rockefeller. Esther, the Finnish cook, who was assigned to show me my household duties, pointed it out to me on a mirrored wall of Mrs. Rockefeller's dressing room. It was his graduation picture from Deerfield Academy, Esther told me, and I can remember how impressed I was by his clean good looks and his kind, brown, almond-shaped eyes. I believe I decided right then and there that someday that face would love me.

The photograph was one reason why I enjoyed dusting Mrs. Rockefeller's dressing room, but it wasn't long before I started feeling a strange, claustrophobic sensation in my own room, which was much smaller and more drab than any I had ever been in. And although my bathroom was far more impressive than what I'd been used to on Borøya, it was shared by three other members of the staff, who apparently took their evening rest in there. The hall leading into the staff rooms was long, narrow, dark, and foreboding, with *nothing* on the walls. Perhaps it was the complete contrast with the family's home that made the servants' quarters gloomy. Whenever I opened the door between the two areas, I had the feeling that someone was saying, "Let there be light; and there was light."

Among the things that impressed me most were a great array of paintings and a number of illuminated cases containing sculptures and ceramics and the like, which beckoned to everyone who passed by. It so happened that, during all the eleven months of my employment, most of the times I saw Mr. Rockefeller he was moving or rearranging, or giving orders about moving or rearranging, objects from his art collection. This was done frequently, and always with a great flourish of excitement that made every change a ceremony. And I soon learned that whatever I liked or admired in those cases or on the walls I had better enjoy while I could, because it would soon be replaced by something entirely different in size and shape and color.

Most amazing to me at the time was the collection of "primitives," as I heard Mr. Rockefeller call them. They reminded me of pictures of the starving heathens I had seen and pitied in my family's missionary magazines, and of the idols from which the missionaries were trying to save the heathens. I was also embarrassed because so many of the sculptures and pictures Mr. Rockefeller carried around were nude. What immoral society could call it art? What unknown reason could this famous family have for owning such pieces, which were everywhere waiting to be dusted?

The family usually spent the weekends at Pocantico, but when they were at home in New York the help were summoned here and there by a bell in the pantry. Each morning we all tiptoed around until the bells began to ring from the various and separate bedrooms. I remember writing home about this fantastic system, and my discovery that *all* wealthy people (in America such a short time, and already I was generalizing) had their own separate bedroom and private bath. It must be wonderful, except if you were in love!

The butler and the waitress were summoned to the dining room by a beautiful, delicate, but very soft bell, and we all seemed to spend a great deal of time just being quiet so we could hear the bell if it rang. I thought at first that the whole routine was ingenious, and designed to give the Rockefeller family the ultimate in luxury. Strangely enough, though, they didn't seem any happier or more relaxed in the morning than the early-rising, hard-working islanders back home. And many times the children in the family didn't get to the dining room on time and ended up eating in the kitchen, just like the help.

Mamma wrote frequent long letters, almost booklets, which carried me emotionally home each time. As I read them I could almost see Mamma, in her clean cotton dress protected by one of those aprons that set the pace for fashion on the island, where patterns for aprons changed much more often than those for dresses. I wrote back: "Mamma, your food is so much better than what the Rockefellers are eating. . . . I am trying to be nice and behave myself, because your eyes are on me wherever I am. I don't know why. Stop looking, please!"

I really did think of my parents and my sister often, drinking coffee and enjoying those wonderful homemade baked goods. Here on Fifth Avenue, coffee was served only in the morning, at breakfast, usually only one cup, and after dinner, in tiny cups that looked like the toy ones in my playhouse back home. Apparently, drinking coffee did not give wealthy Americans the pleasure it gives Norwegians, who drink it every chance they get. As for cakes and cookies, they were occasionally served for dessert, or for "tea" when elegant ladies came to visit Mrs. Rockefeller. The cakes were always sliced thinly, and all food was served on beautiful silver or china plates. Everything would be artistically arranged; the composition was always a masterpiece, sometimes surpassing the cakes and cookies themselves.

No one ever just dropped in on the Rockefellers. Everyone

who wanted to visit any member of the family made a "date," which Mrs. Bay carefully recorded in a leather engagement book. When guests arrived, I often observed them exchanging kisses on the cheek as they exchanged polite small talk. The conversations I overheard then, and took part in later when I was a member of the family, seldom or never penetrated to the personal level. If there were any problems, any fierce inward struggles, they never rose to the surface. The Rockefellers' façade, their public as well as their private demeanor, was constant, controlled, and unchangeable. I don't believe I ever witnessed any anger or tears, any emotional outbursts whatever, throughout the time of my employment.

On the other hand the family was aware, in the broader and more intellectual sense, of all the suffering in the world. They were deeply concerned about underprivileged people everywhere. They spoke sadly and with compassion about young Americans who couldn't afford or didn't receive good educations. They were on a constant hunt for information, gathering bits and pieces from newspapers and broadcasts, and from long and involved but always polite discussions; they paid vast sums for research projects; they read great quantities of books and magazines. They seemed obsessed with responsibility, and the scale and scope of their charitable expenditures are public knowledge.

This social concern was passed on to the younger generation. They were always reading or studying. They, too, cared intensely, and involved themselves in a host of interests outside the immediate family. Maybe they had so much time left over to feel responsible for humanity in general because so many of us took care of their daily comforts. Those children were loved and worried over by Mrs. Rockefeller and, when she was away, by her secretary, not to mention all the members of the staff. Nothing less than perfection would do, and the children's rooms, awaiting their return at any time of the day or night, were always as flawless as we could keep them.

But some of the children had an uncommonly strong love for their dogs, an unusual attachment to animals in general. I could understand loving an animal as I had loved my sheep and cats on Borøya, but it had never occurred to me to take any of them into my room. Here, in this elegant family, the dogs would often sleep in the same bedroom as their owners, and sometimes when I went into a young Rockefeller's room I would have to hold my nose. I couldn't understand what was wrong with their sense of smell, or how Mrs. Rockefeller could allow her children to share their bedrooms with dogs—especially since her delicate touch of fresh flowers was also in those rooms.

Let me add, in all honesty, that for years now I've had a dog of my own, a Chinese Shih-Tzu named He-She. Perhaps because of her Oriental ancestry she seems to understand me. She gives me unreserved devotion and loyalty, responds to my sporadic love, and is always there when I need her. She sleeps next to my bed, in her own custom-built four-poster. And when she had puppies, I sometimes found myself holding my nose again. I have come, it seems, to share the possibly neurotic attachment of Americans to their dogs.

When I first began to know the young Rockefellers I found them puzzling. They had all the money they could ever use, they had so much help and care that they didn't have to do a thing if they chose not to, and yet they were far from my preconceived picture of the happy-go-lucky idle rich. Indeed, I later came to realize that in some areas they were actually impoverished.

Once, when I got up enough courage to be curious with Steven, I asked him how and where he had spent the happiest summer of his life. I imagined an exotic place somewhere in the sun, or being with someone special and famous. Steven didn't have much difficulty deciding, or need to pause long before telling me the tale of his summers at the ranch in Jackson Hole, Wyoming, that belonged to his grandfather, John D. Rockefeller, Jr. His parents had given him permission to stay with the J.Y. Ranch's foreman, Red, and his wife, Belle. Steven worked from early morning until late at night doing any job Red asked him in his earthy vernacular, from which Steven promptly began to enrich his own vocabulary. (He told me with great joy and humor how his older brother, Rodman, had reacted to expletives right off the ranch, and how fast he had put a stop to the new speech pattern.) The most meaningful part of Steven's summer, however, was the fact that he ate every meal in the small kitchen with the couple. Belle prepared all the food, and even washed and ironed Steven's dirty clothes. Her competence seemed to amaze him. He told me that if he ever got married he would spend his honeymoon at the J.Y. Ranch, where he had truly been at peace with the world, where life was simple and fun, and where the beauty of nature was all around.

While he was telling me these things my thoughts wandered back to that formal circular dining room in New York City, and I really couldn't understand why Steven had been so happy at the ranch. I contrasted my picture of Belle, in her tiny kitchen, with Mary Todhunter Clark Rockefeller, beautiful, stately, always serene and gracious. There was no doubt in my mind that she was the epitome of womanhood, and that she organized things and conducted herself in a way that I could hope to emulate only in my dreams.

I recall an incident that made me realize how accustomed she was to having her meals as gracefully served as they were well prepared. One day Esther told me I was to have the privilege and opportunity of completely planning and preparing Sunday dinner for Mr. and Mrs. Rockefeller, who were expected back from the country in the early evening. I thought I did a fine job with the cooking itself and with every other detail, even to the setting of the table with the proper linen, flatware, and silver candlesticks. Seven o'clock came, seven-thirty, eight o'clock. I began to get impatient. I finally stopped counting the times I had lighted and blown out the candles. I had a date at nine o'clock to go to a Norwegian party in Brooklyn, with a Norwegian boy, and a handsome one at that! Okay. At nine o'clock I blew out the candles for the final time and left my proud culinary accomplishment on the very old-fashioned stove. My evening in Brooklyn was filled with fun and laughter, and I was comfortable being with people who understood me so easily. I didn't think any more about my employers who hadn't come to dinner.

The following morning Mrs. Rockefeller came directly to me first, and not to Esther.

"Anne-Marie, what happened to you last night?" I explained the situation as best I could, but she admonished me by saying, "Don't ever do that again! I had to take my husband to Hamburger Heaven on Madison Avenue."

I explained plaintively that it had been Norway's Independence Day and I hadn't wanted to miss an important party in Brooklyn. She reminded me that it was part of my job to serve as well as prepare the food, and to remain on duty until everything was cleared up for the evening. I didn't feel hurt or chastised by her comment; I only mused how good life is for some people. Hamburger Heaven sounded like a great place to me, and now that I knew it was good enough for my employers, I couldn't wait to ask that same nice Norwegian to take me there, too.

In any event, Mrs. Rockefeller dropped the matter. She sat down at the kitchen table shortly after to plan another day's menu with the cook. Esther seemed to stand as straight as a soldier in the German Army when Mrs. Rockefeller was speaking to her, and it made me nervous just to watch the two of them together. They appeared to be acting in a play in which, I felt, I too had a role. Esther was old-fashioned and tried to instill the same type of discipline in all of us. The family was treated, in fact, as I imagined royalty in Norway was.

I liked and respected Mrs. Rockefeller immensely, but she has always filled me with awe. Whenever I spoke to her while I was in her employ, I became aware of my lazy posture, because hers was impeccable. I wanted to be totally helpful at all times; I always hoped to take my orders from her personally instead of through the usual chain of command.

I often wondered if she needed all of us so much and how important to her we really were. I wondered if she knew we were not eating as well as she was. All food looked and tasted good to me, so I wouldn't have been so aware of the discrepancy if Esther hadn't constantly said, "Don't touch this" and "Don't eat that, it is only for the family." I questioned how enormous their wealth could be if they couldn't buy enough of the same quality of food for all of us. But I never thought of complaining directly to Mrs. Rockefeller, because I didn't want to displease her in any way. She was just that kind of person. She never demanded as much from me as I wanted to give her.

I was always aware of her special and superior nature. When I did something improperly, I was twice as ashamed if she found out. Once I answered the telephone when there was no one else at home. Frightened, but with efficiency, I said, "Rockefeller's President." From the throat clearing on the other end of the line I knew I had said something wrong. I didn't mind the little teasing I received from Margaret, the red-haired Irish waitress, when I told her about the way I answered the phone, but I did mind that Mrs. Rockefeller would know, since the call was for her.

Mrs. Rockefeller must have taken my mistakes in her stride, but I took them to heart.

Another one of my embarrassing moments occurred one evening when I was left at home alone. (There always had to be one of the staff on duty to answer the phone.) I was particularly thirsty that evening, and went searching through the pantry for something to drink. Esther had told me many times to drink water when I was thirsty, but I decided to look in the refrigerator, which was an antique like the stove, for something that wouldn't be missed. I found a half-opened bottle of something that looked like soda pop, and drank it. It tasted awful, and I was certain I had been poisoned. I found a doctor's number and called. Excitedly but carefully I spelled out t-o-n-i-c w-a-t-e-r, and asked him if I was going to die. He tried to explain to me what a mix was. I was just glad that I wasn't going to die in my tiny maid's room, all alone, after taking something I had no right to in the first place.

Time passed, and my performance as a domestic improved. Soon winter came, and I had been away from Norway long enough to appreciate the crisp air and the snow. On one of my days off I decided to rent a pair of cross-country skis at a ski shop. I put them on in front of the apartment and skied through Central Park, up through Harlem, which didn't appear as dangerous as my uncle had led me to expect, all the way to 171st and Broadway, where I had coffee and cakes with a Norwegian lady friend I had made. I didn't tell her my means of transportation, which I left in the lobby of her apartment building. I arrived back home at midnight, thoroughly but healthfully exhausted. When I told the story to my uncle later, he looked at me fiercely and said, "If you ever pull a stunt like that again, I'll send you back home on the first boat." I never did try it again. I do believe he meant what he said.

Little by little I made friends in the city. Besides my

relatives, there were the service-elevator men, who took out the garbage, and all sorts of interesting people with whom I could engage in an understandable English conversation. My first dates were with two young Norwegians, one of whom I had known since I was a little girl; the other I had met on the ship to America. They both took me to Radio City Music Hall to see *High Society*.

With my new exposures came a deeper appreciation of the bewildering family I was living with. Whenever anyone discovered where I worked I would be given an opinion or asked questions regarding the Rockefellers. I didn't understand how everyone could know so much about such a very private and quiet family. Even my father would write me news of them. How did he know so much more than I did? Everyone was curious to know what it was like inside their home, or what "living like a Rockefeller" was *really* like. I was amused by an anecdote Steven told me about Rodman after we were married. Once, when Rodman was asked how it felt to be a Rockefeller, he replied, "I really couldn't tell you, as I've never been anything else."

I can never pretend to know or grasp what being born a Rockefeller entails, but I did observe at first, and then live through later, the enormous weight and power that name carries. Perhaps they rang their bell for us, but it became increasingly clear how many people "rang" for them. *Everybody* reacted, one way or another, to their name.

Four months had now passed. I was soon to spend my first Christmas away from home. Part of my joy that year was being invited to the Rockefellers' front-hall sitting room to see their Christmas tree, which was large and grossly overdecorated, and being greeted and thanked by each member of the family personally. I fondly remember greeting Mr. Steven, who still had the special look I had now memorized from his photograph. All the help were given envelopes with money in them. Mine contained ten dollars, which I still have. (Esther told me confidentially that if I stayed another year it would be twenty.) We were all wished a "Merry Christmas and thanks from Mr. and Mrs. Nelson A. Rockefeller," in writing on the envelopes.

All around me the extravagance was overwhelming. I didn't know how to absorb everything I had witnessed so briefly. Later that evening, after I'd had supper with my aunt and uncle, I came back to my room early and wrote home: "I had a nice Christmas Eve, but I wept until my pillow was soaked, although I do not know why. . . . Divide all my kisses equally to only those you know I love."

Whenever I am reminded that it takes the Rockefellers three days to open all their presents, I fondly remember what Christmas was like in my childhood, with its hope, anticipation, and simplicity, and feel sad that my children will never know that experience, no matter how hard I may try to duplicate it.

The young Rockefellers went back to their respective schools, and Mr. and Mrs. Rockefeller went back to their busy everyday schedules, pausing periodically to rest at various retreats they also called home. One such place was Pocantico Hills Estate, in North Tarrytown, New York.

All I knew about Pocantico was that once and sometimes twice a week a man from the estate would come to deliver eggs, cream, milk, vegetables, and cut flowers and potted plants to the city, so I thought it must be some kind of a farm. In the spring I was told that the entire New York City staff, except for Mrs. Bay, would accompany the family to Tarrytown, and then to Seal Harbor, Maine, for the rest of the summer. The apartment in the city was left in such a way that I felt as if we were never coming back. The furniture was fitted with slip covers, and the important pieces of art were put into a special closet in the penthouse, to which, I was told, only Mr. Rockefeller had a key. But we left my little room on the twelfth floor exactly as it was. I began to look forward to the journey. The Rockefellers' chauffeur came to pick up "the group" in a long, red Ford station wagon. Then, on the way up, I wondered and worried about what my chores would be on the farm.

I was surprised when our car approached an impressive twenty-foot iron gate and the Swedish driver announced that we had arrived. I didn't see one thing resembling the country. A very serious and rather dangerous-looking man with a pistol on his hip went through the ceremony of recording our license number, and then gave John the okay to continue with his load. We drove along a lovely winding road until we came to a large, old-fashioned-looking house. It had separate garages across the road, and the help's quarters were above them.

My room turned out to be cheerful and bright, with a fine view of many big and beautiful trees, some of them varieties I had never seen before. I didn't know then, nor did I care, that my room directly faced Steven's corner bedroom, with only a road and a short distance of lawn in between.

Our daily routine here was similar to that in the city. On our afternoon breaks, however, we were allowed to walk anywhere on the estate as long as we stayed on the roads and didn't interfere with the sacred privacy of any of the other Rockefeller homes.

I began to explore the many acres of the inner estate with the courage and excitement of a Dr. Livingston. I was keenly aware of the contour of everything. Nothing was sharp or displeasing to the eye: all the landscape was soft, rolling, and manicured. It may be true that only God can make a tree, but the Rockefellers must take up where God left off. They seem to know how to perfect nature.

I was certain that Mr. Rockefeller would have part of his art collection out here, but I wasn't prepared for what I saw.

Some of the objects were so large that even he couldn't move them around. There were tremendous masses of polished steel, rocks of some type, and things made of materials I simply couldn't identify. Some pieces had beautifully curved forms resembling children, women, or a family. Some bore no likeness to anything I had ever seen except in my frequent nightmares, but there was one large statue of a woman who looked Norwegian, and I was grateful to that artist for making her body "big and beautiful."

It seemed this man I was working for had more than a passing interest in everything beautiful. It was his passion, his love, his main interest. Most of his outdoor sculpture proudly and majestically looked down on or faced the Hudson. The very first time my eyes caught sight of that river from my vantage point on the estate, my emotions turned head over heels. I hadn't known that anyone could be so fortunate or have captured so much beauty and so much poetic scenery in one place and have kept it all to themselves. They could have called it Eden instead of Pocantico.

I met staff members from the various other households on my expeditions through the estate. They told me about Kykuit, where John D. Rockefeller, Jr., and his wife lived, and where there were so many in help that if I worked in Kykuit—the "Big House"—I wouldn't be able to remember everyone's name. The epithet given the house was no understatement. It was as big as any castle I have ever seen pictured. I couldn't imagine one elderly couple needing all those rooms.

To me there was something almost eerie about the estate. It was so perfect and beautiful, but so still, almost like a graveyard. If I did see anyone, even gardeners or other help, they appeared to be working in reverent silence. Only the help and the dogs made the place seem real. Occasionally I would hear the snap of a golf ball as it was being hit on the golf course, and a soft voice saying "good shot." (I wondered if anyone ever made a bad shot.) The golf course was part of a complex referred to as the "Playhouse." The Playhouse encompassed a Grecian-style indoor pool; a modern, sculptured outdoor pool; indoor and outdoor tennis courts; a Ping-Pong room and a card room; a gymnasium; an automatic bowling alley with English prints on the wall; a sumptuous living room for formal entertaining; and a soda fountain and grill area by the outdoor pool for informal entertaining. These facilities didn't look as if they were used much, but of course this was only a first impression, and none of the young Rockefellers, or cousins, as they call themselves, were home from school yet.

The whole estate seemed to be in the hands of gardeners. There were head gardeners and there were second gardeners, who drove around on constant reconnaissance in order to tell still other gardeners where to go and what to do next. Each tree and bush was given so much attention that I wondered if any of the Rockefellers knew that in most other places these things just grew. I couldn't understand why nature needed so much care.

To me, this paradise on earth was missing one ingredient: someone just sitting there, blissfully happy under any of the trees, whispering words of endearment to someone else.

The most surprising discovery was that Mr. Rockefeller had an adjoining house of his very own, designed by Wallace K. Harrison, who also designed the United Nations buildings in New York. It was five hundred yards away from the house he shared with Mrs. Rockefeller. It had a round living room, three bedrooms, and an outdoor swimming pool. He went there every night, and as far as I knew he never slept in the main house with the family.

Years later the unbelievable happened. Mr. Rockefeller had a hideaway from the estate built for himself, located outside the inner sanctum but still on estate grounds. It was a whole enclave, complete with a unique modern house, a babbling brook directly under the bedroom windows, a lake stocked with bass, a nesting ground for fowl, and a sanctuary for wild life. It also included a few log cabins to remind him of Abraham Lincoln and the good old days in America. This whole area was fenced in, and Mr. Rockefeller and Mr. Moore, the farmer and caretaker, had the only keys. Mr. Moore came regularly to reassure the animals that *they* had found heaven on earth.

Mr. Rockefeller managed somehow to stock this retreat with wall-to-wall art, inside and out, even on the little island in the middle of the pond.

And then, after he married Happy, he had a Japanese tea house that had been built for his mother moved closer to the big house. To it he added an authentic Japanese garden, with a special Zen Buddhist section. It takes one man many hours to keep the stones and gravel properly raked. A renowned Japanese architect said that the garden was as fine as any he had seen in Japan.

I think I understand now why he was forever in search of a new hideaway. Each "simple" retreat ended up by being quite complex; besides, he probably needed more space for his art. He seemed to use so much energy and time creating one perfect spot for relaxation after another that I couldn't imagine how he ever found the time to use any of them to be quiet in!

It was a pleasant surprise when I realized this sedate family did occasionally give a party at the Playhouse or in their private home. The tempo and the mood of the estate changed, and long black cars drove on the roads, and the enormous beauty would be shared briefly by chauffeurs and guests. This estate, with its walls and gates and its self-containment, made the Rockefellers seem to me like self-made islanders cut off from the rest of the world.

While Mr. Rockefeller came and went with his important papers or his briefcase tucked under his arm, Mrs. Rockefeller seemed to be his domestic manager, quietly and tastefully running his different retreats. She gave much of herself to her children. Each one appeared to be special and important to her, and it seemed to me that she was unusually aware of their likes and dislikes, their different personalities and different needs.

As soon as the children arrived home from school we began preparation for our sojourn at Seal Harbor in Maine. This trip didn't seem to be as large a production as the one from New York to Tarrytown. I was quite anxious to see a part of the country that might look like Norway, but it didn't thrill me when the family told me Seal Harbor was on an island, all too suitably called Mount Desert.

There is, though, only one word to describe my first impression of everything at Seal Harbor: breathtaking! The air, the view, the sea, the house—everything was overwhelming. By this time I wasn't greatly surprised when I saw that Mr. Rockefeller's "simple" boathouse was at least in part an art gallery, where the many different boats shared the wall space, the dock, and even the harbor with his omnipresent art.

The young Rockefellers were there, and being in the same house with them every day was exciting for me. The cook mentioned that she knew Mr. Steven and Mr. Michael were especially fond of the dogs, but she found it strange that Steven all of a sudden found it necessary to come into the kitchen all the time to feed and check on the dogs, and to make small talk with the help.

We hadn't been there very long when Mrs. Rockefeller

presented us all with free tickets to the big local event: the annual Fireman's Ball. We were given the evening off, and I was really excited over having a change from my kitchen duties. I washed my hair and brushed it until it was shining. Putting on my favorite dress, I thought I looked rather pretty: not as nice or elegant as Steven's sister Mary, but that didn't matter because she wasn't going to be there. This affair was for the local people and the Rockefeller help.

The dance was loud and noisy, but just being there gave me a sense of excitement. I only hoped Mamma wasn't "watching" me as I tried so desperately to dance. In the midst of the noise I was aware of a strange momentary silence and a surprised look on some of the faces of our group. I looked toward the entrance to the hall. There was Steven Rockefeller.

He came into the hall and went over to an elderly, quiet-looking lady sitting on one of the benches along the wall and asked her to dance. "Why her?" I asked myself as I wondered who she was.

In a very short time, while I was having difficulty dancing with an unattractive Swedish man, Steven politely cut in. By this time I was having as much trouble with my respiration as I was with my dancing, so I didn't try too much in the line of conversation. I was relieved when the music stopped and Steven asked me to have a cup of coffee in the basement with the rest of the people. Coffee was just what I needed after some confusing moments in that small and stuffy hall.

• 3 •

Mount Desert

I was relieved when it was time for the music and dancing to end. I had danced very little before, and learning the two-step, or fox trot, as Steven called it, produced a state of nervousness as well as guilt, because I kept remembering Mamma's warnings against dancing. Although I wished these uncomfortable feelings would go away, I didn't want my evening with this charming man to end. The whole event began to seem like an overdramatized fairy tale in which the kitchen maid was about to return to her rightful place by the hearth. It didn't help to overhear two other members of the staff joking with each other. "Mrs. Rockefeller must have given her son a free ticket, too," one of them said. "But you can bet Anne-Marie won't be getting any invitations to the Seal Harbor Club."

Maybe Steven also overheard comments like that, or maybe he just sensed my uneasiness. Anyway, to my surprise, he asked to drive me home. But on second thought it didn't sound too preposterous to me—after all, we were going to the same place. I did think it was at least a slight gamble, though. I didn't have a checking account—in fact I had never heard of such a thing—and the only money I had was in my little Norwegian sealskin coin purse. That probably wasn't even enough for a one-way fare back to Manhattan if Mrs. Rockefeller suggested such a journey. After all, she might not be delighted if she found out that her son had driven me home from a local dance. As if reading my mind, Steven assured me himself that he would see to it that there were no embarrassing consequences for me.

The car we drove home in was not exactly a chariot; in fact it was a rather beat-up old Ford convertible. But it had a good radio, which was probably worth more than the car, and the music was pleasant and quiet after all the noise in the dance hall. Steven told me some of his favorite songs were "Pennies from Heaven," "The Best Things in Life Are Free," and "Making Whoopee." I thought that "whoopee" must either mean babies or money, and decided I'd better not ask which. We took the long way back and stopped by Northeast Harbor. It was most romantic, with twinkling lights and well-maintained boats and a dock where we sat for hours. I had been to harbors in the moonlight before, but never had I experienced such gentlemanly behavior from my escorts at that hour in the morning. Steven talked very seriously almost the whole time! Mamma used to tell me how a good boy should treat me—how he should respect me. In some ways I wanted to believe she was right in thinking that my earlier dates had probably been too hot-blooded and uncontrolled, though I have to admit those nice Norwegian boys hadn't seemed that way to me at the time. Now here I was with this warm, quiet, soft-spoken man, who approached me as if I were the perfect jewel, though one who had everything to polish, including the English language.

From my first hours with him I felt that I was both a challenge to him and his full-time student, rather than just a date. The time went so fast I couldn't believe how late it was when we finally left that spot, where I'd had the most bewildering but delightful experience I'd known until then.

I soon learned that I was indeed like a precious jewel—one that isn't always worn or seen, one that for obvious reasons has to be kept hidden away. I understood perfectly well that in front of Steven's parents and the servants I was to keep my respectful distance, but doing so was often confusing and painful. Sometimes I wondered if the whole dock episode had been no more than a dream, like those I used to have on Borøya. The more he avoided me, the more I thought of him as he had been on the night of the Fireman's Ball, and how he had held me close while we were dancing. The more hours in a day that I had to keep my feelings and emotions locked up, the more intense they became. I was really infatuated with Steven, and began to imagine him as some kind of perfect human being, not just handsome and proper, but nicer and more intellectual than anybody I had ever met. Yet I began to feel that something ominous and sad had slipped into my formerly carefree and uncomplicated existence. My ambivalence only drove me into thinking more and more about those few shared hours. I wanted, needed, and expected more—but more of what, I couldn't really be sure.

After many casual, accidental, and intentional glances back and forth, and other nonverbal contacts, Steven asked to see me again alone and secretly.

One evening I lingered a long time in the kitchen, putting every last dish carefully in place for the next busy day. Finally, after everyone else had gone, I walked down to the boathouse to meet Steven. This time, as a change from the beat-up Ford, we planned to use his father's sailboat *Nirvana* as our hiding place. I kept watching his arms as he rowed us out to the mooring. They looked almost as strong as a fisherman's. I went on sitting in the rowboat, shyly, feeling a bit frightened, as Steven came to me after tying it up. He smiled as he helped me on board *Nirvana* and told me I reminded him of another blond-haired, blue-eyed girl he knew, who seemed outgoing and relaxed and yet blushed almost as much as I was blushing at the prospect of a kiss. I was just receiving that first tender yet strong embrace from Steven when we heard someone approaching across the water. It was Mr. Rockefeller's captain, Marvin Bryant, coming to check on *Nirvana*, because he had seen lights going erratically off and on from the boathouse. Steven, who gave him some short and simple explanation, seemed to handle the loyal old sea captain with characteristic politeness and even some humor—a combination that apparently persuaded him not to bring the matter to Mr. Rockefeller's attention. After Captain Bryant left, the evening slipped by rapidly, and we didn't leave for shore until sunrise. I had to be back in the good old kitchen by 7:00 A.M. to help Gerda Byskata, the Seal Harbor cook—who, like Esther in New York, was Finnish.

Before we left each other we made plans to meet again the following evening. So began the confusing pattern: kitchen maid by day, and by night, secretly, romantic girl in love. It was a bit wearing, but somehow when one is young and infatuated one doesn't count the hours of sleep or show signs of sleeplessness. Sometimes the days would seem long and the work boring, certainly compared with what the Rockefeller children were doing. When I would see Steven and he acknowledged me only by smiling or a brief "Hi"—and this often happened—depression hit me suddenly and hard. It was not a reassuring arrangement, and there was no one at all to share either my anxiety or my happiness. Eventually our long evening hours of talking, driving, petting, and hiding tired me out mentally, emotionally, physically. I finally gave up, telling myself just to trust, believe in, and live for my times with Steven.

Often during those times we discussed each other's likes and dislikes. Steven carefully articulated his in long, detailed, and fascinating speeches. I wasn't too good at expressing my needs verbally, not so much because I hadn't yet grown used to speaking English as because I'd never even thought in this manner, but I seemed to possess enough feelings for both of us.

One night, when Mr. and Mrs. Rockefeller were going to be out sailing for the whole evening, Steven surprised me by inviting me to see some slides of Japan and Africa and other parts of the world he and his family had visited. The screen was set up in the recreation room, and I enjoyed the slides even though they were not exactly well organized and Steven wasn't exactly expert at showing them. In a way, temples resting on their sides and animals that were upside down were all the more interesting! Later we both felt thirsty, and Steven automatically rang for the butler. When slim, stiff-backed Charles entered he seemed shocked to find me sitting with Steven in the family's quarters. I could feel his animosity and disdain. I don't think he had ever liked me, even to begin with, and I always attributed this to the fact that he was Swedish. (The Swedes and the Norwegians have never been the best of friends.) When he handed me my glass of ginger ale and it was only about half full, Steven asked him if he would be kind enough to fill it up. I pictured Charles going back with a full report about me and "Mr. Steven" to the rest of the staff, and I knew then I was in for a tense breakfast with all of them next morning.

However, not even Charles could dampen my good feeling about sitting next to Steven in his home that evening. After Charles left the room, we got into a discussion of Norwegian sailboats. Steven thought I would know about the handmade Norwegian boat his father owned, the *International*, but the boats I knew were used for fishing or work. About pleasure boats I didn't know much more, I told him, than that his father and mother were having their turn at a midnight sail. Suddenly we heard Mrs. Rockefeller's strong but cultivated voice say, "Steven, how kind of you to show Anne-Marie our slides. Goodnight, Steven. Goodnight, Anne-Marie."

I could have passed out. But it was typical of Mrs. Rockefeller to have ended our evening together with such finesse.

After that we were less cautious, and relaxed our secrecy to a point at which we began to discuss our roles in this game of hide-and-seek. Seal Harbor couldn't be called a swinging place, and our comings and goings were surely noticed. One morning Gerda Byskata, who had been off for a weekend, took me into her bedroom. She showed me a large and beautiful embroidery kit for a needlepoint design based on the story of Cinderella, and announced that if and when my marriage took place it would be mine. Gerda seemed more aware of what was going on between us than we were ourselves. This woman was very kind and helpful to me, as protective as a mother. She made me smile when she observed that even if nothing finally came of the relationship between Steven and me, at least the dogs had been getting extra good care since the first day that Steven had taken notice of me in the kitchen.

One evening there seemed to be a disturbance at the dinner table. Something tense was obviously going on among Steven, his father, and his sister Mary. I couldn't hear what they were saying, but raised voices at the dinner table were so extraordinary that I became apprehensive, feeling sure it had something to do with me. I suspected he was being advised not to see me any more, either in public or in private, and when he didn't meet me that evening down by the boathouse I was certain. Very, very late, he came and knocked at my bedroom window. Calmly he told me about the family disagreement, which, after all, had nothing to do with me, and explained how, when he felt unfairly judged by his father, he went off to be alone in the woods. How good it made me feel to think he would come to me for comfort—and, more important, that he believed I might understand him. I climbed out my window, and we shared another beautiful evening in the convertible listening to music and looking at the ocean.

The night ended in a burst of laughter when I explained that it was getting late and that before I changed into my uniform I wanted to take a douche—because, in Norwegian, *dusj* means shower! Steven suggested I'd better look the word up in my Norwegian-English dictionary.

I suppose I did give Steven many reasons and occasions for laughing out loud, something that didn't happen very often, it seemed to me, in the Rockefeller household. In fact, the only criticism I received for the way I did my job that summer was that my loud laugh had evidently disturbed Mr. Rockefeller *early* in the morning on several occasions. He complained to Mrs. Rockefeller, who told Gerda, who told me, and because this came from the "big" boss I took the warning seriously.

Soon it was time to pack up the house and travel back to New York. The ending of any summer is a bit sad, and when the future may change one's good summer feelings or place them in jeopardy, it's harder to accept its demise. Summer has always been a special time for me, when my emotions have been buoyed and protected by the season's freedom, warmth, and undemanding pace. Now I would have to start over, on new grounds fraught with busy schedules, walls, security guards, and that world of society full of bright, young, intelligent, and wealthy people. All this seemed very threatening to me.

Strangely enough, though, the return from Seal Harbor to Pocantico Hills Estate went better than I had imagined, especially within the gates. The grounds were certainly large enough and unused enough to afford us as much privacy as Mount Desert Island or the whole of Arcadia National Park, and we managed quite well to continue our undercover romance. Steven could still come and throw pebbles at my window over the garage; and his bedroom was on the first floor, which made climbing in and out easy for both of us.

One day we were sitting in Steven's bedroom. There was a knock on the door and Michael's voice calling "Chief." (They had called each other and their father "Chief" or "Chiefy" ever since the African trip.) Steven told me to go into the closet, where I spent some long nervous moments, which seemed like hours, among the smelly boots. Michael didn't seem in a hurry to leave.

He and Steven were very close. In fact, if Steven admired anyone it was Michael, with his eagerness, his enthusiasm, and the relaxed way he took life in general. Of all the Rockefeller children, it was Michael who seemed outgoing and energetic like his father.

Hiding in the closet, I could tell when he began to notice Steven's uneasiness, and I could hear him probing for reasons. But Steven didn't really respond to his questions and finally he left, probably thinking his brother was just in one of his quiet philosophical moods that day. I was relieved to come out of the stuffy closet, and I told Steven that I couldn't bear the "suspension" much longer.

He loved my many Norwegian-English mistakes. He told me more than once how my so-called naturalness and my heavy accent made me unique and different. But being called different didn't exactly strike me as a compliment. His whole family used such good grammar, had such large vocabularies, and spoke in a way that I couldn't possibly achieve no matter how long I lived; this made me feel very awkward at times. I tried to believe that I wasn't doing too badly—and I consoled myself by thinking that working in their kitchen wasn't like attending Princeton University, either.

As I look back now I can see that this was Steven's period of rebellion. He questioned his parents' way of life and their values, especially those of his strong and accomplished father. This was something I simply couldn't understand. I had left home to find a better life, but Steven had had that good life from the day he was born, and I sometimes wondered if he hadn't been spoiled by all the advantages he'd enjoyed. But now I can see that the problem of personal identity and the fear of taking on adult responsibilities are part of growing up for every young person—and that problem and that fear become even more complicated and awesome if you happen to be a Rockefeller.

Our worries were never on the same level. Steven was constantly involved in some esoteric or philosophical dilemma, and many times I couldn't grasp what he was talking about. My problems were usually of a physical, material, or tangible nature, or arose from the indefinable feeling of loneliness and melancholia that has been part of my personality from childhood.

It was coincidence that brought me into Steven's life at a time when he was taking a good look at the rigidity and the layers of propriety that go hand in hand with being born a Rockefeller. These real or assumed demands seemed to him like shackles holding him back from most of the small and simple joys of life. To him I appeared completely free of these constrictions. The fact that I was in no way like anything owned, possessed, or loved by Mr. Rockefeller must have been (I can now see clearly) a great attraction for Steven.

Even then, of course, I worried about his reasons for dating me. He was always very honest in telling me that he did *not* love me, although maybe someday he could learn to.

I didn't press him for a commitment, for fear of losing him. Instead, I used a soft hand, a gentle stroke, a smile, or a loud laugh to help Steven forget who he was and what I wasn't. These happy, carefree moments were precious to us both, and I concentrated on them.

One evening I noticed that he was getting ready to go out. He had to take a trip into New York City, he told me, but he wouldn't be away very long. He had a new expression on his face, almost sad and so new that I thought the summer was finally and belatedly coming to an end. I had a feeling he was going to see his girl friend from Vassar whom he'd dated for two years before this summer. My imagination went wild as I cleaned up the kitchen and fed the dogs. After that I set the cook's hair. (Anna, the Tarrytown cook, was German, and the only word for her hair is "impossible.") Then I went to my room in a state of subdued panic.

Much later I heard my name being called underneath my window, but I just pulled down my shade and ignored his calls, feeling rejected and sorry for myself. Next morning while I was supposed to be cleaning his room, he left the breakfast table temporarily and came in to speak to me. I told him I could accept his going out with someone else but I thought he had added insult to injury by wanting me to see him afterward! He looked quite dear as he quietly and calmly told me he actually had seen the girl from Vassar—in order to tell her personally about his new relationship with me, which meant the end of their dating. He seemed to care enough about her to be honest. It was a surprise to hear him admit how close he and I had grown. All kinds of emotions began to well up inside me. It was an awkward time and place for such a disclosure. But Steven gave me a big hug and left, while I finished cleaning his rooms.

That day, late in August 1957, I wrote home to Pappa and Mamma. I explained that I was dating one of the Rockefeller sons but that I didn't expect anything to come of it. I said that Steven was a human being of the finest caliber, by either American or Norwegian standards.

New York
1957

Dear Mamma and Pappa,

Do not worry about the name. I promise you, he is not a playboy. This is not his basic nature—I can tell from our discussions. Only one worry—he takes his life and himself much too seriously. I almost feel pity for him. He is a young person who is desperately looking for a meaning and purpose in life—if there are such things (I surely have not found them). Who knows?

I am very impressed with his manners, which I do not believe are put on merely to be impressive. He is that way with the rest of the workers. For some reason, I almost regret meeting him. Perhaps it is my turn to get a broken heart—I am afraid I left a few around myself.

Mamma, you have always told me not to play with people's affections. I agree, but it can and does happen so easily. It is easy to be in control and be detached from another's feelings if he doesn't really matter.

I am grateful to you both for the kind of life that you had together and shared with Torhild and me. You were never afraid of getting yourself tired physically. Perhaps that saved you from experiencing this mental tiredness which is something I couldn't possibly describe or write about in words. I can only think and feel.

Love,
Your Mia

We enjoyed our last few days on the estate together. It no longer seemed as important to be furtive, and Steven was more relaxed. He even suggested a hike together one afternoon, and we walked over to the farm barns. I was amused and surprised to see what a Rockefeller calls a stable, for it looked like a castle with a cobblestone interior and exterior. Steven told me that his grandmother, Mrs. John D. Rockefeller, Jr., used to sit on a park bench at the riding ring to watch all the grandchildren perform, and hand out ribbons regardless of their degree of proficiency. I thought it rather wise of his grandmother to make all the Rockefeller grandchildren feel like winners!

As we were talking, Steven noticed that I was picking some autumn leaves off the trees while I walked along the path. He stopped me abruptly and gave me a severe scolding, wondering out loud what would happen to the poor trees if everyone did what I'd just been doing. I was amazed. I thought he was being rather silly. After all, few of the Rockefellers ever rode horseback on these trails, and even fewer took walks along them or would feel like picking off or smelling a few fall leaves. They had so many better places to walk, and so very many better things to hold and feel and smell. It was one of those times, and eventually there were many, when Steven confused me with his suddenly pedantic manner. It didn't occur to him that he might have hurt my feelings. He made me feel destructive, selfish, and terribly limited.

I remembered that lecture from Steven on an occasion, after we were married, when the "brothers"—and everyone else on the estate—were deeply concerned because the aging John D., Jr., often driven around in horse and buggy, would request that certain trees be cut down. I'm sure they believed—though they never admitted this out loud—that anyone who picks leaves off trees is simple-minded and anyone who cuts trees down is a victim of advancing senility.

We had many close moments, to be sure—times when we were just Anne-Marie and Steven, two young people attracted to each other, intrepid in our exploration of each other's feelings and bodies. But in matters of the mind and social intercourse, we were both right out of *Pygmalion*. At first I minded that, but it became easier as time went on, and I can remember that I finally even thought how sweet a compliment it was when Steven called me his "fair lady."

Our time at Pocantico ended. We returned to the apartment in the city, and Steven left for his senior year at

Princeton. It was difficult being a maid in his home when he was there, but in his absence it became unbearable. I felt hurt that I didn't hear from him right away, although I knew he couldn't ask to speak to me on the telephone when he had finished talking to "Mother" or "Chief." But then his first letter came, with a picture of Maine enclosed, and what a comfort it was (even if Mrs. Bay, who as Mrs. Rockefeller's secretary seemed to notice everything, remarked that the writing on the envelope looked exactly like Mr. Steven's!). "Summer is a memory which I shall not forget," he wrote. "I am sorry that we had to slip around, afraid to be seen, but even that had its good moments."

After a few more letters—and the time between them seemed like an eternity—I decided that I couldn't go on having any kind of relationship with Steven unless I left my job with his parents. I approached Mrs. Rockefeller and told her of my decision. She appeared to be more understanding about my desire for a new position than I had expected. I felt she was genuinely sad to see me leave. And she gave me a beautiful recommendation ending, "Everyone here loves Anne-Marie, especially the children."

With this glowing tribute I set out in the fall of 1957 to keep from becoming homeless and jobless. First I found a room at 173rd and Broadway. Then I went to the personnel department at Bloomingdale's and applied for a job as a sales clerk. I didn't show them my letter from Mrs. Rockefeller because I didn't think the fact that her children loved me would give me an edge over any other applicants. The man who interviewed me seemed interested, but was hesitant because of my English. With a lot of courage I announced that if I didn't do well selling he could put me in the gift-wrapping section, where I wouldn't have to speak to anybody. But he gave me a chance to sell in the lingerie department, and I didn't have any difficulty. After a while I even did some modeling of the merchandise.

Bloomingdale's was quite a change from 810 Fifth

Avenue. There were as many sizes and shapes of people and as many varied personalities as the mind could imagine. Steven didn't object to my new job, but he wasn't too enthusiastic, either. He didn't have any better suggestions, though, and my emerging independence was good for both of us. It enabled him to call me more frequently, and occasionally I would telephone him, but less often than I wanted to, mostly because he seemed embarrassed, hesitant, and reserved whenever I did. Evidently he enjoyed our conversations only when he could be completely alone on his end of the line and I was alone on mine. He even tried to explain to me how uncomfortable he felt whenever he spoke to me in front of anyone else.

In late fall he wrote that the college was to be shut down because of a flu epidemic and asked if I'd like to come to Princeton for a weekend. I couldn't believe that I was about to have my public debut as Steven's date. I bought some new clothes and excitedly called Uncle Andres and Tante Margit. I thought I could dress at their home and have Steven pick me up there so they could meet him, but they absolutely refused. Uncle Andres, who had been a New York policeman too long to believe that there were any wealthy *gentlemen* left, was sure Steven's intentions on such a weekend would not be all that honorable. It didn't matter to me what Uncle Andres thought, though, and I decided it would be better to meet Steven downtown anyway. I took a subway to Ninety-sixth Street and came up out of the exit into a pouring rain. All I could think about, even after I'd climbed into Steven's same old beat-up Ford, was the state of my new clothes and how bedraggled and wet I would still look when we arrived at the university.

The campus was beautiful, but Steven's room suggested that neatness was not a virtue Princeton seemed to be cultivating. My next stop was the house where I would spend the two nights that I was there, presided over by a

Princeton lady who like others of her kind rented rooms to students for their dates. A few more girls were staying in the same house, and others had rooms at Ivy, which was Steven's eating club. These girls were nothing like any Norwegians I had ever known, but they weren't like Mary or Ann Rockefeller, either. And I don't think any of them shopped at Bloomingdale's. They were all attractive, thin, and well dressed, with lots of clothes and jewelry that they changed as often as Nelson Rockefeller changed his paintings. Everyone talked endlessly about clothes, boys, and other dates, which campuses were better than others, and similar topics designed to display one-upmanship. But I did meet two people who seemed just a little more real, down to earth, and warm than the rest. Both are still my friends today, and one is helping me make this book possible.

The eating club was rather formal and reminded me somewhat of the estate. The men dined by candlelight shining down from silver candelabra. Everyone called Steven "Rocks," which for some strange reason made me very uneasy. He was president of the club, and one of his jobs was to check all of the rooms after a party to be sure everyone had gone. Upon deciding that one of the upstairs rooms was vacant, he called to me to join him there. We sat down, pleased at last to have some privacy—only to discover, after a little while, that another couple also thought they were alone. Steven was shocked and upset, especially when it became evident that the other man was one of his good friends. Ever after, his clubmate could get to Steven by saying *"Jeg elsker deg,"* probably because they were three words Steven could not bring himself to say to me (or to anyone) in either English or Norwegian.

I was also taken to visit Dr. Hadley Cantril, a scientist Steven admired very much, who was most pleasant and cordial, and asked me ever so many questions as he gave us a tour of his laboratory. Afterward Steven seemed pleased, as though I had received a stamp of approval from his professor. He told me that President Eisenhower and Walt Disney had both recently visited the lab, and that the President wasn't too pleased with Cantril's "tricks" but that Walt Disney kept his sense of humor. I know now that Hadley Cantril was a student of human behavior; looking back on the incident, I'm glad I wasn't aware at the time of the implications of all his silly questions.

When I got back to New York, I had so much to think about and sort out for myself. But one thing was sure: I couldn't go through life feeling sorry for myself when Steven's Princeton friends and his family spoke about matters that were beyond my comprehension. To begin with, I decided to take a good basic course in English at Hunter College the next semester. Shortly thereafter, while talking to Steven one evening in a pay-phone booth near my rooming house, I looked across the street just in time to see someone shot dead. It was definitely time to move! I remembered that once when I had gone to church with Gerda, I had met a nice elderly woman friend of hers, Mrs. Mattson. I called her and asked if she could possibly take in a boarder. She seemed agreeable, so I moved my few belongings to her home on Summit Avenue in the Bronx.

Bloomingdale's became more hectic, and more lonely, too, as Christmas approached. At the end of one day, tired and hungry, I found myself with only a dime and a subway token in my pocket. I used the dime to call Mrs. Mattson. Apparently Steven was home for the holidays and had called to invite me to dinner. I approached the first man I saw and asked if he could change the token for a dime. He just smiled, gave me a quarter, and told me to keep the change. When I called the Rockefeller home, I discovered that I was invited to dinner *with* Steven's parents. Their apartment was close enough for me to walk to, and I was hungry enough to accept eagerly. We had a nice evening, and although his parents were formal they were also cordial. My only problem was that I was starved, and when I saw what small portions Mrs. Rockefeller took I decided to do the same, trying my best to be a lady. I thought, perhaps she eats seconds. But no! No seconds for anybody except Steven. I left the table only slightly less hungry than when I'd arrived. Steven drove me home afterward and seemed pleased that the evening had gone so well. When we reached Mrs. Mattson's, he gave me a huge package from the back of the car. I invited him in, and gave him the Norwegian sweater I had knitted for him for Christmas. Wishfully thinking that a ring would come in a small box, I was not terribly excited about my own big present, though I had never seen such a large package. And when I opened it, I was literally speechless: inside was a life-sized stuffed penguin! I had never heard of a grownup giving a toy to another grownup, and I couldn't understand why Steven had chosen such a strange gift, or guess if it was meant as some kind of secret message.

As usual, I spent the Christmas holidays at Tante Margit's and Uncle Andres'. When they asked me what the present from "my" Mr. Rockefeller had been and I told them, my aunt knowingly said that that was the kind of thing people gave each other in this country when they couldn't give anything personal. My aunt had a way with her words that reached right into my most private fears. It was lonely enough that I wished I were with Steven and wanted just a little warmth. I went over to Uncle Andres to snuggle on his lap, only to hear Tante Margit's voice snap, in broken English, "Don't you have enough with one man?"

I went home feeling miserable, and fell asleep with my penguin and Steven's Christmas card, depicting a stained-glass window, thinking that at least the card had a religious message.

Steven had enlisted in the Army, and after the holidays

went to Fort Dix, New Jersey, for basic training. His letters were frequent, full of news, and almost lighthearted. He wrote and thanked me touchingly for the blue sweater, which seemed to mean a lot to him. I couldn't help smiling once, when he told me he had to write 1,000 times, "I will not drop my rifle." I decided nobody was perfect, and I couldn't understand why they would make Steven perform such a childish task.

He told funny stories about the platoon sergeant, Casanova, and about soldiers who could not perform their duties or who missed their mothers. The stories revealed Steven's sense of humor about himself and his camaraderie with the other men. The only people who irritated him were those who complained about the food. It seemed perfectly good to him, and he found the mess hall a refreshing change of scene from his family's dining rooms or the Ivy Club.

One day Mrs. Rockefeller telephoned me to have a quiet, personal talk, as she would with her own daughters. She seemed concerned about the fact that Steven and I might be dating each other too exclusively. She thought it would be wise for both of us to date others for a while, and just enjoy ourselves, without all the complications that beset a serious relationship. She meant to be kind, but didn't realize how advice to someone so young might be taken. I immediately wondered if she wanted me to break up with Steven and if this was how it was to end, or if she was showing genuine concern for me as a daughter. She wanted me to think about the serious and necessary social adjustments I was making, and would have to continue to make, in order to fit into Steven's world and his life. She had another piece of motherly advice: the sweater I'd worn when I was last in her company was too tight. I shouldn't wear such clothes if I didn't want to give people wrong ideas about what kind of girl I was. As for herself, she confessed that she regarded me as an honest individual who was being nothing but straightforward with her son. A thought flashed through my mind that she had no cause to worry about Steven's behavior, whether or not I wore a tight sweater.

After the conversation ended, I thought how much concern and courage it must have taken for her to discuss all these personal things with me. A mental image of her in her loose silk blouse tucked neatly in to her tailored skirt passed through my mind, and I began to cry. Then I wrapped the pretty sweater to send home to Norway, where sweaters are for keeping warm and not for giving wrong ideas.

In truth, most of what Mrs. Rockefeller had told me was very important. I thought she was right, and I tried dating a few other men, one of whom happened to be a close friend of Steven's. He was kind, thoughtful, and seemingly interested in me. Naïvely, I would report all of my activities to Steven, who didn't approve at all, feeling that at any moment I might lose my self-respect. I also enrolled in some dancing classes, about which Steven also had misgivings, because I wrote to him that I sometimes danced with older men there. He just didn't trust older men with young women, even in a dancing class!

We discussed my new social role over the phone and in many long letters. Steven was becoming more and more interested in me, and protective to the point that I felt I belonged to him. So I found it increasingly hard to comprehend his reluctance to become intimately involved with me. But he asked me what I thought would happen if a Rockefeller ever got a girl pregnant. Then he told me this had actually happened to a member of his family, and it had taught him a lesson he never forgot.

One night he took me to see *Song of Norway*, with music by Edward Grieg, at an amphitheater on Long Island, and on our way back to the Bronx he managed to get lost. In some ways I did not mind, because Mrs. Mattson was away and I was returning only to an empty apartment. As we kept making wrong turns, I tried to look as upset as he, but inside I was happy just to be in his company. It was only when we had nearly reached Mrs. Mattson's that he surprised me by announcing that he had a toothbrush in his pocket and if I wanted him to spend the night he could; but he quickly added that he would be proper and not do anything that would embarrass me or upset Mrs. Mattson.

This Rockefeller tradition of propriety was beginning to get me down! We didn't sleep much that night; instead, we had many hours of probing conversation. I became stubborn, because in no way could I get Steven to speak of his love for me. He just kept repeating, "Perhaps I could learn to love you!" Maybe he was only being honest, but honesty in such a large dose is sometimes hard to swallow. What he said and what I felt with him were two different things. I began to get an urge to return to Norway and forget about America and Steven Rockefeller as well.

As predicted, Mr. Rockefeller was going to run for the governorship of the state of New York, in the fall of 1958. Steven pitched in and was busy with all sorts of things in his father's campaign. It was quite exciting to see the family's name in the *Daily News*. (I still had not progressed to the formidable New York *Times*.) But the publicity, too, began to have its anxieties for me. Every now and then there would be a column about Nelson's eligible son that pictured him as a scion of great wealth, flirting with society women and hat-check girls. I was jealous and upset, even though I could not bring myself to believe that any of the stories were true. I don't think Steven would have been upset, except that he was still involved with Fort Dix and was trying every way he could to make the men—and himself—forget he was a Rockefeller. Now he feared this notoriety would result in his getting preferential treatment. One day, sure enough, there was Steven's picture right on the front page: ROCKY'S SON IN

THE ARMY, or something to that effect. Poor guy! A uniform that was too big for him and a woebegone expression made him look like someone to be saved by the Salvation Army rather than Nelson's son in the United States Army.

I received calls and telegrams from all the places he went with his father. One day he called to tell me a joke. It appeared that Senator Keating, who was also campaigning, rinsed his hair with a raw egg every day, but on that particular morning, room service had presented him with a fried egg. Steven thought he had to share that marvelous joke with me immediately. Not knowing Senator Keating well, remembering how on Borøya an egg twice a week was a real treat, and not even having an extra egg to eat at the moment, I wasn't convulsed with laughter. I just said, "That's funny, Steven." When I got off the phone, I remembered having approached a total stranger a few days before, to ask him if he would be so kind as to buy me a plate of baked beans at Horn and Hardart!

Mr. Rockefeller was duly elected governor in November, and Steven regarded his father's honor with solemnity and such a strong sense of responsibility that he questioned the meaning, purpose, and direction of his life over and over again. His search for some new but previously hidden meaning seemed painful, exciting, and necessary.

Off and on I began to not feel well, and I was pleasantly surprised by an invitation to go to Florida with an elderly childless couple who had always been kind to me while I lived with Mrs. Mattson. So I spent two weeks in Palm Beach that winter. While I was away, Steven called and wrote to me often. He seemed to be missing me, and he looked forward to my return.

We made plans to meet at the airport, and I imagined he would pick me up in the familiar old Ford. But he hadn't been feeling too well, either, he told me—not well enough to drive himself. So he led me out to a car with faithful John behind the wheel. John was one of the few members of the Rockefeller staff who really liked me, and who, unlike most of the servants, spoke in the same tone whether he was addressing me or "Mr. Steven."

We drove to 810 Fifth Avenue, where we went to Steven's quarters until dinner. I was feeling tired and nervous, and really not paying too much attention to what he was saying, when I was astonished to hear him ask me how I would like to be his wife. At first I laughed, thinking this must be due to *his* sickness. And then I hugged him, which was the only answer I could give at the moment. Whatever Mr. and Mrs. Rockefeller thought or knew about us at that moment, they kept their opinions to themselves. However, Governor Rockefeller took me by complete surprise as I was about to leave after dinner. Without letting anyone else become aware of the fact, he pressed something into my hand. It was puzzling to open the beautiful box and find an exquisite jade necklace. Later, the Governor told me it was part of an Oriental jewelry collection made by his aunt, Lucy Aldrich Rockefeller—a real character, he also confided, who used to return from the Orient with all kinds of *objets d'art* tucked in her bra and other clothing.

On the weekend we went to the estate. Sunday afternoon Steven suggested that we go for a walk and do a little bird watching. All of a sudden, about ten minutes after we had started out, he thought he heard a pileated woodpecker, and, as he excitedly pulled me with him, he mumbled something about telling the Audubon Society. We came to a large swampy area, where he gallantly carried me on his back, but we never did find the bird, because his back began to hurt. I felt awful, thinking my weight must have injured him. He was in pain all evening and the next morning, too, before he left for Fort Dix.

Not long after I got back to the Bronx, Mrs. Rockefeller telephoned to report that Steven was in the Army hospital with an undiagnosed illness. Immediately I wired him two dozen American Beauty roses. I wanted to go that very day to see him, but he wrote that I should wait until he was feeling better. By now they had discovered that he had pneumonia.

When it was finally time for me to go see him, Steven cautioned me about the ride on the bus, which might be filled with soldiers returning from leave. Neither the bus nor the PX was a safe place for a single girl, he told me. But when I boarded the bus, the person who sat next to me was a friendly and chatty woman who told me that Governor Rockefeller's son was in the hospital with her son, and how everyone there thought Steven was such a nice, unspoiled young man. She was even bringing him some cookies.

The first thing I saw, inside the hospital room, was my bouquet of red roses, which looked somewhat out of place in that depressing cubicle. Steven himself looked pale and thin, and I wanted desperately to hug him, but the only thing I could think of saying was, "Steven, your pajamas aren't pressed!" After all his protestations, he was evidently happy to see me. We talked about his back trouble, which he believed had been caused by his carrying me, and about the roses. He said I should forget his previous concern about writing too frequently for fear that someone would notice my return address and find out about us. He told me to write as often as I wished, but I needn't put my name or address on the envelope, since he knew both.

On the bus ride home, I realized the extent to which I cared for him, and wondered if I was going to keep my balance—if it wouldn't be better to go back home to Norway and find someone who would "learn to love" me faster. I tried to make myself believe that everything at home would be different now, anyway. Three years after I had left for the United States, my father decided to retire, and he and my mother moved to the mainland, to a little place called Lohne, in the district of Søgne. So it wouldn't be as if I were going all the way back to Borøya.

By now, though, I was beginning to feel really sick all

over—tired, aching, and generally just not myself. After Steven and I discussed this, he asked Mrs. Rockefeller to make an appointment with a woman doctor for me. I had every kind of a test, and not one showed anything organically wrong. Finally, when the doctor had finished her examination and had begun to talk to me, I started to cry and tell her that my disease was "love sickness." When I was through she just nodded, and agreed that a trip home might be exactly what I needed.

Since my visit to the doctor had been suggested by Steven and his mother, I had been under the illusion that Mrs. Rockefeller would pay for it, but I was wrong! I learned that I owed the doctor seventy-five dollars for listening to me tell her that I was in love. There was nothing to do except admit I didn't have the money to pay her at the moment. Later, after we had become engaged, I imagined reading in the papers about how Steven Rockefeller's fiancée didn't pay her bill. The matter wasn't settled, in fact, until September 1959, when I sent the doctor a check signed "Anne-Marie R. Rockefeller."

The day I left New York City in the late spring of 1959 was an especially poignant one for me. Steven wouldn't come to the pier to say good-bye because my aunt and uncle, who still didn't trust him, would be there. He tentatively promised to land in Norway someday, and maybe then, maybe there, we would have no more painful good-byes.

I made every effort to forget him as soon as I was aboard ship, but in vain. My evenings were filled with melodramatic thoughts about star-crossed lovers and impossible dreams.

The day the ship landed in Norway I purposely put on the navy-blue gabardine suit that Mamma and Pappa had bought for me to travel to America in. I didn't even use lipstick. I didn't want them to think that I would come home like an overdecorated Christmas tree just because I had been to New York. When we reached my parents' new home in

Lohne, there were a surprising number of anxious letters from Steven.

One letter told me how he felt trapped, to a certain degree, by his name, by publicity, and by the various ventures in which he was currently engaged, looking everywhere for some kind of balance. Perhaps I could provide this balance? His last day in the Army was to be July 9, and after attending the wedding of his friends Bob and Martha, he planned to leave for Norway. The fact that I was gone had come as a sudden shock to him. He told me of the hours he had spent thinking about our relationship, and as time went on he would write more about this to me. He told me quite honestly that I was the first and only girl for whom he had cared and whom he wished to be kind to. The realization was coming to him how much he *loved* and missed me. My heartbeat and my body were not functioning properly. Reluctantly I answered the letters, which contained all the thoughts and feelings that I had hoped to hear for three years. Without realizing that I was doing it, I apologized in advance for my small home and my simple family. His assurances came back immediately: there was nothing more relaxing to him than the thought of being in simple surroundings with good, honest, and basic people. The size of a house or how fancy it was meant very little to him. He told me that a man may have lived all of his life in one small place but understand certain primary truths about life that another far more experienced person may never have grasped. It was as if he were telling me that many people read volumes of books and remain ignorant.

He assured me that the language would be less of a problem for him than I might expect because he had started listening to Norwegian-language records while he was in the Army, and now he was studying with the help of records that promised he could learn Norwegian. The letters became more and more tender and romantic. His favorite song was now "My Happiness," by Connie Francis, because it reminded him of me. This surprised me because not too long ago he would have considered such a blatantly sentimental song as bordering on bad taste.

On June 2, I received a letter that said, "P.S. Let's get married on August 15. XOX."

Evidently Steven had gone home to Tarrytown to see the family. In the course of a weekend he told those closest to him that he would be going to Norway, and that he would quite possibly marry Anne-Marie. He wished them to be prepared in case the press might approach any of them. No one was shocked. His sister Mary had been expecting the news, and his Uncle Laurance said that the ranch in Jackson Hole would be free from August 15 through September 1 and we were welcome to use it for our honeymoon.

We made plans to meet at the Oslo airport, and Steven cautioned me that if he was a bit reserved when he greeted me it would be to avoid a public display of emotion that could lead any reporters that might be on hand to draw their own premature conclusions. And if by chance a reporter should question me before he arrived, I was to just say that Steven and I were friends. I was also to be very cordial, because "reporters have the last say."

I put on my loveliest Norwegian everyday costume, which I had bought in Oslo, and set off to meet him. Mamma and Pappa were not too enthusiastic about my friendship with this young man, especially now that our seemingly sudden and serious interest in each other might result in engagement or marriage. But even though they were worried, they, too, began to get excited about his arrival.

At the airport I didn't notice or think about anyone except Steven. When he came from the plane, looking cheerful, relaxed, and happy, I was amazed that he had finally arrived. One of his first remarks was: "I'm sure I saw your island as we were coming in!" I said that was hard to believe—there were so many islands that even I couldn't pick out my own from a fast-moving plane. I went on feeling excited, and the more we talked the more anxious I became for him to meet my family. He was so marvelous then that I couldn't imagine how *anyone* could fail to approve of him. And if they did, I wouldn't care.

He told me he had been thinking how much fun it would be to travel to Kristiansand S by motorcycle. It seems he had always had a desire to drive one, but hadn't been able to imagine a Rockefeller in a black leather jacket and motorcycle boots roaring around New York City. Now he was becoming "unfettered" very quickly. Before I knew what was happening he had bought jeans and kidney belts for both of us, and then he bought a motorcycle. When he found out that before he could drive it he had to get a special license, he began to seem a little nervous. But he got the license, and before long we set off.

He tried to impress me with his newly discovered skill, but the roads in Norway are sandy, narrow, and bumpy. We had a slight accident, and I received two bad burns, which he doctored for me. Then we got a flat tire and had to have a new one sent from Oslo by bus. This took several hours, and we were both getting tired and hungry. Fortunately I saw some blueberries a few feet back from the road, and went to pick them. Steven was most impressed with my ability to provide!

After we got under way again I just held on tightly to his waist, alternately wishing we would never reach Søgne and praying we would get there in one piece. When we did eventually arrive, my parents just stared at my quiet, soft gentleman from America, who was not at all like the image of him that they and my sister had made in their minds. He did not look anything like a playboy.

ILLUSIONS

• 4 •

On becoming
Mrs. Steven Clark Rockefeller

Soon Steven was fully accepted as part of our small household. His thoughtful though halting Norwegian made Pappa feel at ease. His silent grace before meals and the gusto with which he ate endeared him to Mamma, who asked him to call her by her first name. Never before had she been so verbally appreciated. "Thank you, Lovise, for the delicious dinner." "Thank you, Lovise, for making my bed." There was no end to his gratitude for things that Mamma had done all her life for everybody. Torhild and I were relieved that Steven actually found it rather delightful to wait his turn for our only bathroom. I was made to feel embarrassed about just one thing in our home. He couldn't understand why Mamma had such an abundance of sentimental religious pictures everywhere, especially in the bedroom. They made him feel as uncomfortable as I did when I first encountered Nelson's nudes.

By degrees, Steven met the relatives, all of whom invited us to come by for coffee and cakes. One day Steven said we had to do something about this hospitality. He'd had thirteen cups of coffee, an equal number of *kaker*, and three full-sized Norwegian meals that day. There are some fortunate people who always make a good first impression, and Steven was one of them. His strong and sure handshake just made people feel friendly toward him, and it disarmed those who equated wealth with weakness or lack of manliness. But a little cousin of mine didn't understand that Steven came from a wealthy family. He whispered to me how sorry he felt for my new boy friend, who had to wear sneakers with holes all over them. Not even the poorest Norwegian would be seen with such torn shoes, and Jan Rudolf felt tempted to buy Steven some new ones so he wouldn't embarrass me in front of the other relatives.

My favorite uncle, Mamma's youngest brother, Magne, felt that Steven was a kindred spirit in his appreciation of nature, and offered to take us up into the valley to visit Mina Solaas, known as Mina *på Bakken*, a woman who supplied him with some of his firewood. I cringed. "Mina on the Hill" was well known locally. She was a recluse who had never married, and managed a farm in an area rugged enough to tax any man. Occasionally she would hire drifters or poor souls who were down and out, but that was more to help them than for her own sake. Mina's face showed the effects of many hard winters, and looked wizened the way an apple does when it begins to dry. She had very few teeth. Her body was old and bent like a mountain troll's, but very strong, with hands that were gnarled and three times the size of mine. But her most distinctive characteristic was her voice, which invaded one's eardrums the way chalk does when it screeches across a blackboard.

All of this intrigued Steven, who wished to set out to meet Mina as soon as possible. He and Uncle Magne and I trekked into the valley, and, just as I'd predicted, we could hear her and smell the farm—all the livestock, pigs and cows and sheep and horses—long before we got there. As we approached the old lady I had to smile to myself, thinking that if ever Steven was going to meet someone for whom the name Rockefeller had no meaning, here was his golden opportunity. Predictably, Mina came to her door, greeted us heartily, and offered us the hospitality of her kitchen, where she promptly heated up some thick black coffee and opened up a large brown sack filled with old bread. Every week Mina made a trip into town to buy old bread from her favorite bakery, and she saved it up in her sack as a treat for her animals or unexpected guests. She believed that old bread was much more healthy—and my mother does, too, to this day.

The few primitive pieces that furnished the kitchen looked as carved and weathered and old as Mina. She poured our coffee into cups, of a sort, that looked as though they had never been washed. My piece of bread felt like a stone, and I just fidgeted with it, looking for an opportunity to drop it under the table for some grateful cat. But Steven followed Uncle Magne's example, dunked it in his coffee, ate it with relish, and then asked for more. I was sure, from the pleased look on his face, that he was thinking to himself that at last he was with a *real* Viking. We chatted a while, and Mina said she wouldn't change places with anyone, nor would she have wanted any other kind of life if she could have started over again.

Outside the house, underneath the barn, Uncle Magne spotted a plow that must have been three or four hundred years old, and he made some remarks about its value to Mina, who was quite aware of its worth. She picked it up and handed it to him as a gift. Being a shrewd businessman, Uncle Magne whispered to me, "How much do you think Steven will pay for this, eh?" I was furious that a member of my own family would suggest taking advantage of Steven like this. But Uncle Magne was a great tease, and in addition to his business sense he had a strong sense of humor. He later gave the plow to Steven as a present. Years later, at the time of our separation and subsequent divorce, it was one of the items Steven designated as being of personal importance to him.

On the way home we made a slight detour, and stopped at the farm of another of Magne's cronies. This aging man was being cared for by his longtime housekeeper, Hilda, who was just as strong, kind, independent, and untidy as Mina. When we entered their farmhouse we introduced Steven, explaining that he was here from America for a visit. I don't know if it was Steven's name or his country that prompted the woman to run and fetch a plaque bearing a citation from King Haakon VII of Norway. She proudly explained that this had been presented to her for her devotion and loyalty to her employer. How senile the farmer now was seemed questionable when we were leaving and he wondered out loud, "If this is a Rockefeller here in my humble home, you may have the farm—but first, if you are a Rockefeller, where is your diamond ring?"

Another day I took Steven out to Borøya in my father's fishing boat. He loved my childhood home. A noted author from Oslo, Odd Hølaås, was living there now.

So far everything and everyone in Norway delighted Steven. He answered many questions about America, and he listened to and was fascinated by whatever people said, whether it was day-to-day gossip or talk about religion or politics, the mainstays of any Norwegian conversation. He made everyone feel his own worth and dignity—traits I believe, from what he told me about his Grandmother Rockefeller, that he must have inherited from her.

One day he heard that a horse was mired in a ditch and that many men were unable to get the poor thing out. This touched his strong humanitarian side, and off he took on his motorcycle to see if he could help. The exhausted animal must have made one valiant effort just as Steven pulled on the rope, because out it came. He was the hero of the day, and his strength and his way with animals grew more remarkable every time the story was told. (But when he fell off a large work horse he was trying to ride, no one paid much attention.)

A few grumbles filtered back to us from some of the husbands in the area who were tired of hearing how young Rockefeller did grocery shopping and dishwashing for Lovise and ran errands for Mia, and being asked, if a millionaire took over such domestic chores, why couldn't they?

Everything about the trip seemed to be going so smoothly that I wondered why Steven had said nothing about our engagement and marriage since the last letter I'd received from him. Finally, one day I just confronted him with the subject. I also decided that I would go alone to visit an old friend on a farm in Søgne. Steven followed me to the farm and asked me to come back again, because he had something to tell me. He confessed then that he had been carrying the ring everywhere with him since leaving home. At one point, he said, he'd been tempted to ask Pappa to take him out in his boat so he could throw the ring into the North Sea: he had a premonition that if he did that he would spare us both a lot of future sadness. But later, he told me, he decided he could not go back to New York without me, or turn away from the prospect of a simple, natural life in a cozy home with meals planned, prepared, and served by me. He then presented me with the lovely ring. It was understated and plain, with a small diamond, but to me this long-awaited gift was the most precious and significant I had ever received.

Steven had many requests to make about our life together, but only one of them was easy: we would not have any servants, at least in the beginning, because he wanted us to start off like any other couple—doing our own planning and painting and fixing, and getting to know each other in the process, just the two of us, on our own. That sounded like paradise. Otherwise, it appeared, he was going to be my teacher, with the help of his mother. He seemed frustrated and even angry when I refused to say much about our future and what I would be willing to do and not do.

Pappa was thrilled. He said, "This love is something! It seems to be so clean and pure. I only wish I were young again." Torhild didn't have much to say, and Mamma didn't seem really sure, either, even though it was obvious how much she liked Steven. I couldn't tell if this was just part of her lugubrious view of life or if she had genuine doubts about us. Perhaps she was unhappy merely because reporters had started to flock around, some of them not too careful of her beautiful rock garden, trampling the much prized and admired flowers.

She was worrying, too, about all the preparations she would have to make, all the food she would have to cook, for our little informal engagement party the next night. And then we learned that her next to oldest brother had died tragically that very day. My aunt begged us to go ahead with the plans for our party. Hoping it would ease the pain for her and Mamma, we went from the funeral at noon to supper at our house to celebrate my engagement to Steven Rockefeller.

Little did Mamma know that soon there would be nothing at all left growing in our back yard. Word of mouth travels quickly in Norway; and, like a plague of locusts, reporters from all over the world appeared to ask if the news about the engagement was true. When Steven replied yes and someone asked me why I'd kept it secret for so long, I said, "The right time to announce it is after the fact."

The American press and the gossip columns in New York didn't take the whole matter with any great seriousness, and the local papers expressed misgivings about my having been labeled a Norwegian Cinderella. People who lived around Søgne were quoted as wondering if a Rockefeller would be good enough for a Rasmussen (or a Svendsen) whose lineage went back to 1555. Heritage is terribly important to many Norwegians, and by their standards the Rockefellers' wasn't nearly as old or sturdy or pure as the Rasmussens'. It was pointed out, for instance, that there was no German blood in the Rasmussens or the Svendsens, while this was not true of the Rockefellers. One paper even published our entire family tree, which delighted and excited Pappa. He had always wanted to have that information, and now the laborious task had been performed free of charge.

On the very evening our formal engagement became public, we decided to leave Søgne and take a trip on Steven's motorcycle, our only means of transportation that summer. We invited an aunt and uncle who had a car to join us, bringing along Pappa, Mamma, Torhild, and a few cousins. So the whole group followed us, carrying camping equipment, as we left the low-lying southern coast and traveled north into the greener hills and valleys. We found a plain mountain hotel, where everyone registered for the night except Steven and me. We set up our tent next to the hotel. That night we celebrated the engagement again, and then everyone left Steven and me as we zippered ourselves into separate sleeping bags.

The next morning my uncle awakened Steven and told him to hide the motorcycle. Reporters from the New York *Post* were in the area. I went into the hotel to stay with Mamma, and Steven went fishing in a nearby lake with Pappa. They stayed for six hours! Evidently someone had told the reporters about our camping trip and they had set out to look for us. A kind farmer near the hotel told them we had left for home, and when they got back to Søgne a neighbor of ours named Sigrid told them we had gone on to

Oslo. This kept the press on a fine wild-goose chase, and we had another whole day, free from questions, for fun and relaxation.

All of us went hiking that day. We stopped for refreshments at another small hotel, and as we entered, Steven spied a slot machine. He put in one coin—and hit the jackpot! Mamma just shook her head and said, "The rich get richer." Steven's pockets were bulging with coins and he was terribly pleased with himself. But then somebody told him that machines like this one were for the benefit of the Red Cross, and he put back all his winnings, coin by coin, hitting no more jackpots.

On our arrival back home we found the newspapers full of stories about our trip. One paper quoted the Defense Minister, who had seen us whizz by him on our motorcycle, as gleefully hoping that "Steven's millions would follow him into the country." Another paper defended me for going camping with Steven, saying that we were well chaperoned and that camping with a boy is an accepted social custom for Norwegian girls.

One publication noted that my favorite pastime was reading movie magazines. Steven asked me if it was true, and I told him that actually I had never read one in my life. From then on I only translated the parts of the newspaper stories I wanted him to hear.

More reporters in our back yard: "Was this a surprise to you, Steven?"

"Surprise? I've known Anne-Marie for a long time, and have been dating her steadily for over one year."

"How many fish did you catch on your trip, Mr. Rockefeller?"

"I hope I do as well with my marriage as I did with the trout. I caught nine."

"Is fishing your hobby?"

"It used to be. Anne-Marie is my hobby now."

"Anne-Marie, what kind of fish does your fiancé favor?"

"The salmon around Borøya." At least the Norwegians of the Sørlandet would get the joke: there are no salmon around Borøya.

I didn't catch the chic-looking American reporter's message when she asked, "How did it feel to have dishpan hands at 810 Fifth Avenue?" Steven did, though, and his arm tightened a little around my waist, as it did whenever we faced any sort of interview. He always held me protectively and answered most of the questions unless they were specifically directed at me. Now he just asked the woman reporter if she had another question.

"Mr. Rockefeller, why did you major in history at Princeton? Why didn't you study economics, being a Rockefeller?"

"I thought I'd better learn something about the past, because I will have enough to do with economics in the future."

"Anne-Marie, will you go back to the United States to study?"

"I am uncertain of my future plans. I am only sure of one thing, and that is, I can run a home, and run it well. My feet will remain on the ground, no matter what."

"Mr. Rockefeller, how does your family feel about Anne-Marie?"

"My family is happy with the engagement."

So many personal questions. The next morning when we looked out the window and saw two women reporters in sleeping bags by the side of the road, Steven decided it was too much for us to handle, and he telephoned his father for advice. Nelson said he would send Mr. David, a public-relations man who worked for the family in Rockefeller Center, to help us.

That night Mamma thought she heard something in the garden. When Steven looked out and saw a flashlight, he told us to stand back and he would handle whatever it was. It turned out to be only a Danish woman reporter who had decided to spend the night, hoping for some kind of scoop. Steven just asked good-naturedly what a nice woman like her was doing out alone this late at night. So at least one reporter didn't bother us any more.

Nerves were becoming taut, and no one thought it was funny when we were all awakened early the next morning by a constant beep, beep, beep from the motorcycle. We all rushed out only to find that something had happened to the wires. Steven easily took care of that ridiculous crisis, too, but we had just recovered from it when more reporters began surging around us.

"Mrs. Rasmussen, how do you feel about the marriage?"

"It's not easy to give your daughter to a Rockefeller. We have the deepest concern. . . ."

"Mr. Rasmussen, are you happy?"

"We would all have to be fools if we weren't. If these two families do unite and become a reality, rumors, for once, will have spoken the truth."

The constant strain was beginning to tell on all of us, especially Mamma. She announced that she did not wish to see, talk to, or have her picture taken by any more journalists, and she took to hiding, crouching, and running away whenever anyone approached. I talked her out of this to some extent by telling her that the reporters would print things she wouldn't like if she didn't co-operate at least a little.

Pappa seemed to relish the commotion, and we would often find him talking to a reporter the way he would with a customer in his store on Borøya, pipe in hand, extolling the virtues of his family or country. "This Søgne District is marvelous—I've always been happy here, and I love it."

Somehow only Torhild managed to keep her thoughts and life to herself. "How's your sister?" they'd ask her. "Fine, thanks. How is yours?" she'd say. Understandably, she wasn't eagerly sought after as a prime source of newsy tidbits.

Bestefar, too, was mostly left alone. By this time he was so old he existed in another world, where he had an imaginary friendship with Hallesby, a famous Norwegian evangelist. When a group of reporters spotted him one day and one of them recognized him as my grandfather, they all rushed over and asked, "What do you think of him?" He looked up and said, "Oh, you mean Hallesby." But before he could tell them about the virtues of the evangelist, they left him to his solitary chores and imaginings.

Old boy friends, anyone at all I'd ever dated, were pursued for information. "No comment," was what most reporters received. Teachers, friends, and shopkeepers were offered money in exchange for pictures or information. The whole thing was getting out of hand. But Mr. David arrived and arranged for weekly news conferences, and that helped. Mail and presents began to come from all over the world. Every day we made a motorcycle trip to Lunde and picked up two saddlebags full. Most letters were friendly and congratulatory, but a great many also begged for some kind of help—money needed for illnesses, piano lessons, schools. From many places I received claims that someone was my relative. It was very depressing. Steven told me not to worry, that the Rockefeller family was used to receiving all kinds of letters from strangers, and he just forwarded them to a special department at Rockefeller Center that handles such matters.

We didn't have much time for all the decisions and preparations that go into a wedding. First there was the guest list. We hoped to keep it small and simple. Not many of Steven's relatives and friends would actually be coming to Norway. There would be only his parents, his two sisters, his two brothers, who would be ushers, and his four best friends from Princeton: Bob Waldron, David Montgomery, Harold Talbot, and Gerald Rigg, who would be best man. The rest of the list would be composed of my own relatives and other people close to me. Torhild would be my maid of honor, and childhood friends would be my bridesmaids. Admittance to the church would be by invitation only, and it became difficult to limit tickets, as they came to be called, because it turned out that too many people in Norway wanted to receive one.

Steven expressed a desire to be married in the three-century-old church, *Gamlekirken*, in Søgne. It was primitive, tiny, and full of tradition.

"I love that old church, Mia," he told me. But I really wanted to be married in my church, which was new by comparison, where I had been baptized and confirmed. After listening to my reasons, Steven willingly capitulated.

We had another problem. Pappa thought we should import a well-known organist, Bjarne Sløgedal, considered a city slicker by local residents, instead of relying on the regular organist, Hans Skarpeid, who was getting quite old. But so many people were upset by the idea that the old man who had played for everyone's weddings, including Pappa's and Mamma's, and for christenings and funerals as well, might not get to play at our wedding, that Steven and I decided we must use him to keep peace in the valley. We asked him to play the two pieces he performed best, the "Wedding March" from *Lohengrin*, and the "Norwegian Wedding March" by Oscar Borg. Old Hans reminisced about my ill-fated organ lessons and concluded that I could have "gone far" if only I had practiced and continued my studies.

When a reporter asked me about my wedding gown, I hadn't yet decided what I was going to wear. I only knew that I would be a white bride, and that I wanted this to be a Norwegian wedding. In the end the material that appealed to me most was white duchess—imported, I'm sorry to say, from Germany—interwoven with roses that would glitter and shine as I moved. The local seamstress, Mrs. Nygård, had made some pretty dresses for me when I was a child, and I had always been thrilled with what she produced. She was known as never having ruined a piece of material for anyone, and I felt absolute confidence in her now. When pictures of the gown were finally released, I think its simplicity and traditional unsophisticated look disappointed some people, who thought it rather tacky. I received many suggestions, some of them subtle and some obvious, about going to a fancy and exclusive shop in Oslo, "just to see what they have."

Another unexpected complaint came from stores in Kristiansand S selling cosmetics, because many newspapers reported the fact that I wore no make-up at all, and that was having an adverse effect on sales.

When Mrs. Rockefeller arrived, the reporters asked her if she had brought any wedding gifts.

"No, they will be arriving with my husband."

"What did you think of the pictures of Anne-Marie's wedding gown?"

"It would break her heart if she couldn't wear what she had chosen herself."

"Will you be planning the menu for the bridal dinner?"

"No, I'm sure Anne-Marie and Mrs. Rasmussen, being very well organized, have done that already."

Mrs. Rockefeller stayed at the Ernst Hotel but came out to the house to meet the relatives and spend some time with us. The morning after she arrived, while I was packing a picnic lunch for us all, I was annoyed at something and swore in Norwegian. Mrs. Rockefeller said, "How quaint, I just love the sound of that word. What does it mean, Anne-Marie?" I had no trouble making up a polite little lie. Later that afternoon, while she was eating with the rest of us, out of the sedate Mrs. Rockefeller's mouth came a word seldom used even by sailors. She looked proud and pleased about her Norwegian contribution to the conversation, and Mamma just shook her head and glanced at me in bewilderment.

The next arrivals at the airport were Steven's two brothers, Michael and Rodman, and Rodman's wife, Barbara. Barbara's parents were Scandinavian, but she had never been employed as a maid. Seemingly preoccupied with the Rockefeller money and how it was spent, the reporters asked the brothers what they had brought for us. Michael and Rodman replied that it was a Rockefeller custom to see what a couple needed before any gift was purchased. Then Steven's friends arrived, and I began to get as nervous as if the whole Princeton campus were being transferred to Norway.

Soon plans were under way for a good old-fashioned bachelor party, to be held at the hotel, which had already been dubbed "Rockefeller Center." The night of the party I persuaded my girl friend, Kari, to drive me past the Ernst. The whole affair was making me feel most insecure, and I thought perhaps Steven's friends would convince him of his mistake and persuade him to go back to the United States without me. As we drove up to the Ernst we heard noises of the wildest kind of merrymaking. People outside were making comments about Steven and smiling in a way I did not like. I wanted to charge in and beg him to forgo this strange American custom. I also wanted him to get to church tomorrow without feeling ill. But Kari talked me into leaving, telling me it would all be a part of the past in the morning.

I myself didn't feel much better the next day. The first thing that arrived in the morning was my wedding bouquet, chosen by Steven, which contained lilies of the valley and yellow roses. In Norway, I had heard that to receive yellow roses was a bad omen because they signified false intentions. I could only hope people would take into account that Steven wasn't Norwegian.

We also had to hold one last news conference before the ceremony. Steven made a strong and dignified appeal to the journalists and photographers.

"This is a religious occasion and I am not a public figure," he told them. "You represent freedom of the press. I represent something equally important. I represent the privacy of the individual." He also announced that no reporters or photographers would be allowed in the church during the service. Two reporters tried to get around this edict by hiding in the enormous old potbellied stove, but they ended up by terrifying each other, and both of them left in great haste, no doubt feeling that Somebody up there was watching and passing a stern judgment on them.

Steven may not have been a public figure in himself, but his family name and his father were the uppermost topics of conversation on everyone's tongue. Even King Olav V of Norway became a "wedding tragedy." A trip he was taking through the northern part of the country had been front-page news until the Governor arrived. Then the Monarch's journey was abruptly relegated to the back pages. Even when it was falsely reported that President Eisenhower would also attend the ceremony, most people didn't react strongly because the Governor was already excitement enough. If Norwegians could have chosen a new form of government with a president that day, Nelson Rockefeller would have won.

Steven and I, crowds of reporters, and many Norwegians waited at the airport for the plane carrying the Governor and his two daughters, Mary Rockefeller and Ann Pierson. The flight had been somewhat delayed, and the excitement and suspense kept mounting.

When the Governor stepped off the plane at last, waved to the crowd, and shouted, "Hiya, Kids!" he received a thunderous welcome to shouts of "Rockefeller, Rockefeller, Rockefeller!" The shouting probably prevented the reporters from asking *him* about the gifts, which was too bad, because he, at least, hadn't waited to find out what we needed. He brought with him gold cuff links for Steven, a gold Cartier watch for me, a gold mirror for Mamma, a gold lighter for Pappa, and a gold watch for Torhild. The reporters clustered around him and followed all of us to the Ernst Hotel, where we joined the other members of the family and Steven's friends.

The hour for the wedding finally arrived. My legs felt like macaroni, my head was light as thistledown, and my hands were North Sea cold. A certain numbness was a part of my being. I guess I looked rather pale—I learned later that one of the spectators believed my pallor must mean I was pregnant! Voices, questions, people, and noises fell on another layer of me. I moved in some kind of hazy unreality. In this detached manner I managed to dress, join my family, enter the car, and proceed to the church. Evidently it had been raining but had stopped before Pappa and I came out of the house. Even if there had been a downpour, though, I really would not have noticed.

Steven and his mother were waiting up at the altar as Pappa and I entered the church and proceeded down the aisle. I joined Steven, and we both solemnly approached Pastor Gautestad, who gave his wedding message:

Today millions of young people from all over the world are with you who stand before the altar at Søgne parish church. We most cordially wish you happiness on your wedding day, and I pray to God that this day may be the beginning of many days with happiness and the blessings of the Most High.

Love is the greatest adventure in life, and to everybody it is the most wonderful experience. It is a fact that your mutual love has been met with a spontaneous enthusiasm from all over the world because it gives expression to a great thought which impresses everybody.

In our time, when the majority seems to be pleasure-seeking and most youths have film stars of doubtful moral qualities as their

The Rasmussens in 1942:
Lovise and Kristian,
Torhild and Anne-Marie

The Svendsen grandparents with
their three-wheeled motorbike

The house on Borøya

Steven's Deerfield graduation picture, 1954

Anne-Marie at eighteen

Steven and Anne-Marie in Maine, 1957

On Steven's motorcycle, Søgne, Norway, 1959

After the wedding, Søgne, 1959:

Anne-Marie and Steven
in front of their parents;
back row, Rodman C. Rockefeller,
Mary Rockefeller,
Ann Rockefeller Pierson,
Torhild Rasmussen,
Michael Rockefeller

Joseph McKeown, Time/Life

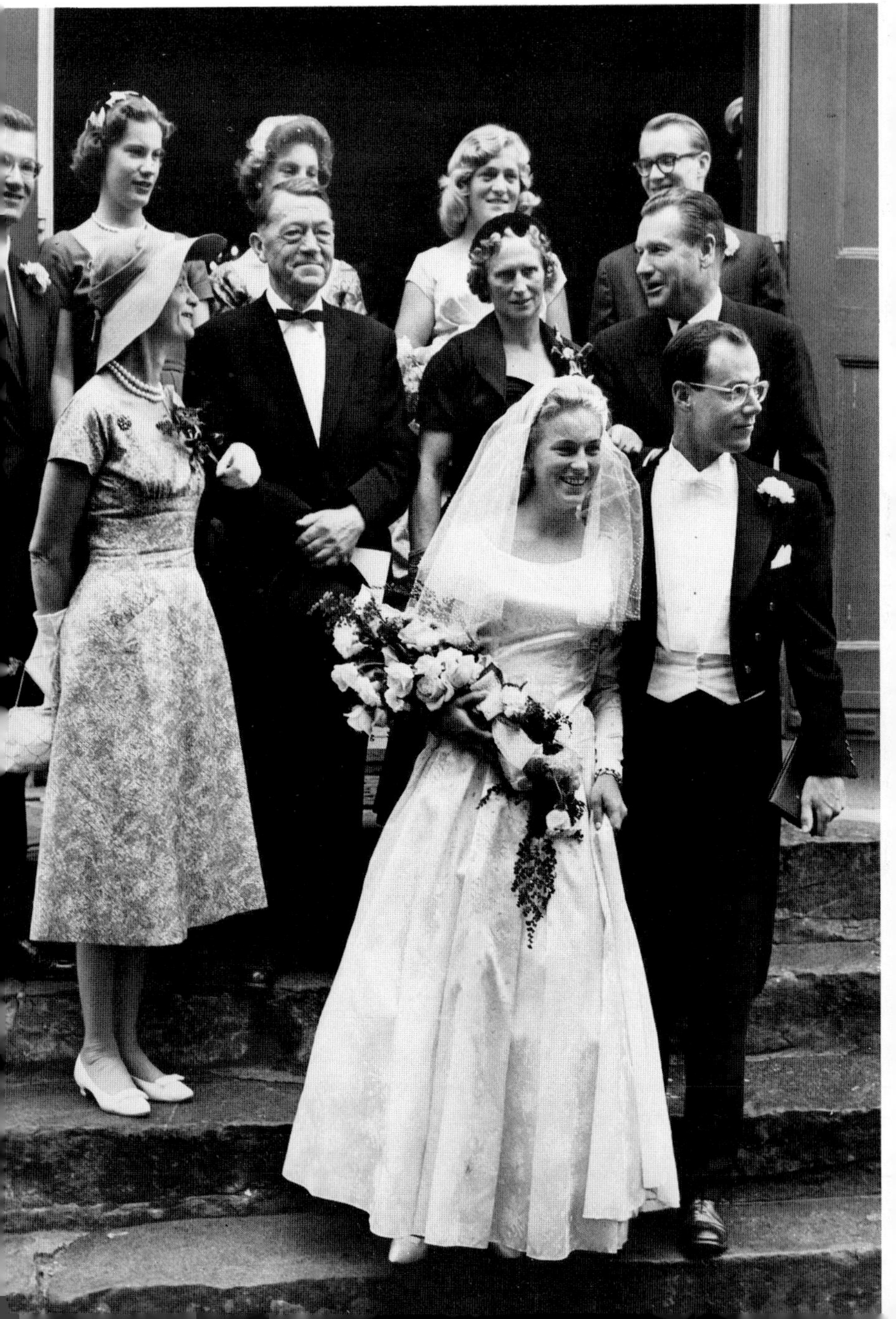

Trygve Lie, Steven, his parents, and Anne-Marie at the wedding reception in Kristiansand S.

The crowd outside the church

Joseph McKeown, Time/Life

Leaving the reception

Anne-Marie's parents
waving good-bye
at the airport
Pierre Boulat, Time/Life

The honeymoon cabin, J. Y. Ranch, Wyoming

Steven and Anne-Marie in Søgne

ideal, the world press has paid tribute to an ordinary girl who has taken pride in being industrious, reliable, faithful—this is the ideal of Christian womanhood.

Therefore it is appropriate today to think with gratitude of the thousands of women who live in accordance with that ideal. Such women are fit to build the new world we are all longing for.

You who stand before the altar today have the best possibilities to build a good home. Both of you have taken good building materials with you from the homes of your childhood.

The first years of your life, Anne-Marie, you spent on the island of Borøya with industrious people who, in order to earn their daily bread, had to fight against the powers of nature. This life formed your soul. All these memories from your island home you will take with you through life as valuable treasures.

Now when you are going to leave your home, your village, and your native country, we thank you for being a good ambassador for Norway, and we hope that you will be a good member of the Rockefeller family and a useful citizen of your new country.

And you, Steven, take with you into your home a good inheritance. We have learned to know your God-fearing nature and the moral qualities inherited from your dear parents.

Your open mind and warm heart and your straightforwardness have appealed to all of us, and in our little village we have come to look upon you as one of our own. You are a fine representative of your family and of the great nation to which you belong.

But a good inheritance is not enough to build a house that can stand against all winds. We are not able to build alone. We must have God with us.

You shall build the house on the rock of the Word, for founded on the rock it does not fall when floods rise and winds blow.

Please remember that your home will set an example to thousands of homes in the States. Let them see a Christian home in which love and willingness to serve naturally belong to life.

But let us never forget that the greatest happiness in life is to have personal belief and trust in Jesus Christ. "What is a man profited, if he shall gain the whole world, and lose his own soul?"

In our wedding rites there is a wonderful sentence which in a way emphasizes the mutual duty of husband and wife: "They shall help one another to come to everlasting life."

We pray that God may bless your marriage from this day on until death do you part.

The pastor then turned to Steven and asked if he would take me as his wife. Steven said, "I do."

As if to compensate for this gentle answer, I almost shouted a strong, firm *"Ja"* when asked if I would take Steven as my husband.

Conforming to Norwegian custom, Jerry Rigg, as best man, had to promise that Steven would be a good provider, brave and strong, like the Vikings of old. Jerry didn't have to wrestle with his conscience too much in making that traditional assurance.

In Norway the groom does not kiss the bride. After we were pronounced man and wife, we led the bridesmaids and ushers down the aisle. As we began to walk, I noticed Pappa, Mamma, my elementary-school teacher, and various friends, some in festive Norwegian costumes. Then I looked to the other side and saw my new American family and, sitting behind the Governor, Trygve Lie, who had been the first Secretary General of the United Nations—the aisle that I was walking along seemed ever so wide.

The ride to the *Klubben*, now jokingly called the "White House" in Kristiansand, which usually takes about twenty-five minutes, took more than an hour because of the crowds along the road. About ten thousand people lined the streets in Kristiansand. Wild cheers greeted the Governor and his family as they emerged from their car, and a phalanx of policemen helped clear a path for them. When Pappa arrived, though, he just used his big Norwegian shoulders to make a way through the crowd for Mamma and himself. The crowd applauded and shouted good wishes to Steven and me. We seemed to be the embodiment of everyone's dreams and hopes, living a fairy tale in which love enables a bride and groom to overcome obstacles, have a beautiful wedding, and live happily ever after. Maybe, too, they believed I had become the richest Norwegian overnight, just like the winner of a sweepstakes or lottery, and they were vicariously sharing my sudden shower of wealth.

The reception went well, with many touching speeches and beautiful songs and poems composed and sung or recited for us by members of the family and other guests, and even by strangers.

Bestefar was seen shaking his three fingers at the Governor. Unable to understand his garbled vocabulary, Nelson sent for the toastmaster, who was Norwegian by heritage and worked in Rockefeller Center. The toastmaster told the Governor that *Bestefar* had been instructed not to chew tobacco today under any circumstances, but he badly wanted to by now, and he wondered if Nelson couldn't help him out. *Bestefar* got his tobacco.

I had several glasses of champagne and felt I needed some assistance in getting to the ladies' room. Kari Hellesjø, who was sitting next to me, got up to help. As we started down the steps, one of the many hoops from my petticoat came undone, rolled across the dance floor, and started down the steps into the lobby. Several excited ladies began to chase after it, thinking they would get the perfect souvenir from the "wedding of the century," when fast-thinking Kari called out and said that it was hers, thereby saving me much embarrassment.

After the reception, the driver of the car took us home via a carefully disguised route. Nobody really expected us to spend our first night as Mr. and Mrs. Rockefeller in my room in Søgne, in a house where my sister and parents were also present.

As we entered the quiet house, my first concern was to see if the rice that Steven's friends had thrown at me as we left the reception had damaged my dress. To my relief it hadn't. But this was another custom unknown in Norway, and I'd been shocked when I saw something being thrown at us. Steven had explained that it was a way of wishing us good luck and happiness—and now the wishes for wedded bliss were all over the room! I set about sweeping them up, because I didn't want any of the rice to get between the sheets on the old sofa that had been made up as a bed for Steven and me: Mamma had washed and boiled them, then dried them on the line.

Neither of us felt very much at ease, knowing my parents and sister were coming home at any minute. As I started to fall asleep in Steven's arms, I could hear him whispering "Mrs. Steven Rockefeller," as though he, too, doubted that he had finally married me. He quickly added that he was happy and proud that I had chosen to become his wife.

The next morning, when I thought of all the new people I would have to meet and all the curious Americans who would be judging me, I looked at Steven and said, "Promise to stay close to me."

As we stood at the airport saying our good-byes to my family, on August 23, 1959, I recalled that it was exactly three years to the day that I had left for America the first time. I was carrying some oak leaves and a few "bought" carnations, which were presented to me by Uncle Magne, who told me, "In case you don't know, those flowers are very expensive." The oak leaves were full of holes from insects—another of Uncle Magne's jokes.

Governor and Mrs. Rockefeller thanked Mamma and Pappa for their hospitality and invited them to come to America so that it could be returned.

Before he boarded the plane, Nelson Rockefeller looked at the people gathered there and said, "Thank you for Anne-Marie." Inside the cabin, he turned to Steven with his typical grin, and asked, "How're you doing, Chiefy?"

• 5 •

Guggen and Guggi Rockefeller

Because of the private compartment, I was not at all aware of the fact that we were on a commercial airline, the Royal Viking Deluxe SAS. We hadn't seemed to be in the air very long when I was told that we would be landing in Copenhagen.

As we stepped out of the airplane, I pointed to the red carpet going down the steps and all the way into the airport and asked Steven what it was for.

"In honor of the Governor of New York," he told me.

It felt as though we were being treated like royalty. We were greeted by airline· officials and prominent political figures, and escorted to a V.I.P. room. The Danes are noted for their hospitality, and I could see why. We were made to feel welcome from the moment we entered the lounge and were asked to sign the guest book. I was given the privilege of signing first, in deference to my being a new bride. When the others had finished, Steven whispered in my ear that it might be wise to add the name Rockefeller after Rasmussen. As I did, it occurred to me that I now had a curiously long signature, but I would never want to drop my maiden name. Perhaps I was for Women's Liberation long before I knew what it meant.

Since our stopover was long enough to afford some shopping time, the rest of the family left to tour the airport terminal. Because of the mobs of people that had gathered to get a glimpse of us, we decided, for safety's sake, to stay in the lounge.

Michael and Mary stayed in Copenhagen, and the rest of the party boarded the plane for America. We had another first-class compartment, with berths that were too close for comfort. I felt terribly shy about climbing into the berth with Steven, because everyone was looking at us with a certain smile—and the smiles came easily, probably due to all the champagne that had flowed in celebration.

Steven fell asleep quickly as I rested in his arms, but even though I was as tired as a sick worm, I lay awake for hours, staring at the moon, which seemed to hang unmoving just outside the window.

Early in the morning I opened my eyes to a large jewelry box that my new father-in-law must have pushed through the curtain. Embarrassed by his generosity and by the whole situation, I fumbled nervously with the box. Inside was a necklace of diamonds, pearls, and sapphires. It surely didn't seem to fit me or anything I had to wear. But Steven explained it was the kind of jewelry that I would keep in a safe-deposit box at Chase Manhattan Bank, as his mother always had done, and might take out just now and then for a dress ball or other grand occasion. I knew Steven didn't like this type of fancy necklace, just as he didn't like fancy corsages. I remembered he'd told me that whenever he had to be an escort at any of the debutante cotillions he would pick his flowers from the flowerpots around the house, much to the consternation of his mother. At the time I, too, thought that was rather stingy, but at last I see the humor in it.

It was difficult to comprehend the meaning or value of all the presents I had received in such a short period. My main concern was how to say thank you from my heart in the proper way, with the proper English. Steven wasn't much help there. He didn't know how to say his thanks on my behalf for the expensive gifts, either.

Shyly, he told me I would receive my wedding present from him in Wyoming, where we would be spending our honeymoon.

Finally our flight came to an end. When we disembarked, we were met by at least fifty reporters and two hundred spectators on the arrival platform. Television cameras zoomed in at us from every direction. Beads of perspiration rolled down my face. A little girl rushed up to greet us with a bouquet of camellias. I was so touched by her and by the exquisite flowers that Steven's taste underwent a change— on many festive occasions, over the years, he gave me camellias to wear instead of home-picked flowers.

In all the confusion I managed to spot Uncle Andres, and I rushed over to give him a "put-on" kiss. I was annoyed at him for not coming to the wedding, and for giving strange interviews to the press about not having been invited or not having enough money to go to Norway. He was also quoted as saying I had never brought Steven around to meet him when I had lived in the Bronx. I remembered all of this, plus the ten-dollar bet he'd made that Steven's intentions would never be serious, as I motioned to the Rockefeller family to come and meet my uncle, the tactless policeman.

Steven: "I'm glad to meet you, sir."

Governor Rockefeller: "I'm sorry you were not at the wedding, it was a beautiful affair."

Uncle Andres: "Well, somebody's got to stay behind in New York."

I could see Uncle Andres' political feelings were about to

surface, and I looked to Steven for help. With a promise to visit my uncle sometime in the near future, Steven steered me toward a waiting limousine driven by John, Mr. and Mrs. Rockefeller's chauffeur. The Governor and his family headed toward another limousine. Except for a few pleasant exchanges with John and some comments about the wedding cake I had carefully carried with me from Søgne, we had very little to say to each other. Cars of photographers and reporters followed us right to the gates of the estate.

The usual maximum security of Pocantico afforded Steven and me a private evening, which we spent in his bedroom. It was nice not to have to climb through the windows.

Steven arranged for one of the family game wardens to meet us at 4:30 in the morning to drive us through the estate to a set of secret gates. From there we used the back roads to the Westchester airport, where the family plane was waiting for us.

We landed at a small airport in Jackson Hole, Wyoming. Red Matthews, still the head foreman of the Rockefeller J.Y. Ranch, drove directly to the plane ramp to pick us up. We traveled by a complicated route, evading anyone who might be trailing us, to the sanctuary of the Rockefeller gates on the ranch.

On the way, Red told us that John D. Rockefeller, Jr., had had a honeymoon cabin built for us on the property but that we "might" have a problem with the plumbing. There was not yet a working toilet, but he assured us that a plumber would arrive at seven the next morning. When I whispered to Steven, "Can't they come a little later?" Steven laughed and Red imitated my accent. A small private joke between them ensued, and I remembered Steven telling me how Red had introduced him to swearing not so many years ago. I could see now how difficult it was for him to complete a sentence without using some profanity. (But Steven told me that in front of John D., Jr., and the ladies Red was discreet.)

With memories of the so-called farm barn and horse stable of Tarrytown, I was unprepared to see a Rockefeller ranch that was just a ranch, and I was equally unprepared for a honeymoon log cabin that turned out to be so primitive.

The large living room had a conspicuous but comfortable bed in the middle of the floor, but the room was so covered with Indian art objects and Navaho blankets that I wondered how (or if!) we would ever get into it.

It all looked so Nordic that I thought the Indians must have stolen their ideas from the Vikings. Steven said that this was an interesting observation, and that if I went to South America I would find similar resemblances, because almost all of the cultures have influenced one another.

There were wild flowers placed all around the room, and that, too, reminded me of home.

Looking into the bathroom, I could see a bent, beat-up ceramic cowboy inside a plastic box, with a sign around his neck that said DON'T OVERDO IT, BUD. DON'T OVERDO IT. In big block letters someone had printed on a sign over the toilet: OUT OF ORDER.

Steven set a match to the fire already laid in the big fireplace, and the room immediately seemed filled with the sound of gunshots. I was frightened because I had never heard a fire do that, even with the wettest of wood. When Steven's cousins asked us about the fire, we learned that they had fastened balloons to strings in the chimney. The only room that didn't seem to present any problems was the kitchen, until I turned from inspecting the refrigerator, stocked with food, and heard Steven excitedly tell me how we would catch fish and cook our own meals. The thought of frying fish on my honeymoon didn't fill me with ecstasy, and I decided a long warm bath was in order, to salve my feelings and calm my confusion. I used some pine bath oil to erase the image of fried fish. The pine odor reminded me of the small scented pillows Mrs. Rockefeller had given to me and all the domestic help as souvenirs from Maine in 1957, and this brought back a flood of memories of that summer. The sensual fragrance and thoughts of Steven melted away my petty annoyances with the American sense of humor regarding marriage and honeymoons. Soon I was snuggling next to Steven in the bed. It was nice to find clean white sheets and pillowcases under the Indian art.

The next morning Steven gave me an antique Navaho necklace he'd purchased some time ago and saved for the girl he would someday marry. It obviously meant a great deal to him. He then produced riding togs for me, and said the time had come to put them on. I'd never worn riding boots before, and he had to laugh when I wobbled, my feet went out from under me, and I slid halfway across the room on one of the Indian rugs. He said I was all set to ride a horse now that I'd taken a fall and learned how to get right back up again.

When we went out to the corral I was horrified to see so many horses confined in one spot. And for some reason Red petrified me—he looked as if he could give one big yell and have the whole herd charging out of the corral to greet me. Instead, he just led up the horse he'd picked out for me. Her name was Duchess, he said. By now I was expecting some kind of joke or embarrassing remark from Red, but, surprisingly, he was gentle and thoughtful, and volunteered to stay close to me on the trail, at least during my first few outings.

I felt so high up on Duchess that I thought it was the closest I had been to God since the airplane journey. Duchess didn't go very fast, but Red was really helpful and reassuring, and it wasn't long before I felt the horse's rhythm and began to gain confidence.

After that first ride I asked Steven if we could take Duchess home to Tarrytown with us. For me she symbolized my first challenge as Steven's bride and how I had met it. But as things turned out, five years passed before Laurance Rockefeller brought Duchess to Pocantico, and by that time I was proficient enough at riding that I didn't want to waste time kicking poor gentle sleepy old Duchess just to get her to move.

The night after our first full day on the ranch, Red got hold of somebody to impersonate a reporter, who came to our cabin door requesting an interview with Mr. Rockefeller. Steven made all kinds of excuses, and when he wouldn't open the door, Red and a group of men and women started banging pots and pans together. It took a long time for me to realize that the pans and lids had nothing to do with Steven's *kitchen* maid. It was just one more old American custom still being carried on out West—a shivaree—as I later learned.

Not long after all this commotion, Steven's cousin Laura, one of Laurance's daughters who was also staying at the ranch, came to speak to me in private. She wanted to know if I needed any information about birth control. Of course she was only trying to be kind and helpful, but I was horrified. The subject hadn't even come up between Steven and me, so how could I possibly discuss it with Laura, who couldn't have too much knowledge to pass along because she had been married only a short time herself? Later, when I told Steven about Laura's delicate diplomatic visit, I said I wasn't up to worrying about such things and just didn't want to discuss them with him or anyone else again. That was one subject I was unwilling to discuss.

During the next few days we hiked along trails Steven remembered happily from previous summers. Some of them he himself had helped clear and keep up. He told me that when he was thirteen the whole family had come to Jackson Hole for a vacation. He had enjoyed himself so much that when it came time to leave, he cried uncontrollably and told his father he wanted to stay, always, at a place where the whole family could be together, far away from New York City or Pocantico Hills or Washington, D.C. He told me that the closeness and understanding he had achieved with his father at that time had hardly been equaled since.

On one of our hikes I picked some wild flowers to make a crown for my head. Steven warned me not to do this, but I remembered the leaf episode and paid no attention. Besides, didn't John D. Rockefeller, Jr., own the land? Well, he had, once upon a time, but he didn't any more, as I found out when a forest ranger approached us with a serious look on his face, wondering out loud why I, of all people, didn't know the rules about picking wild flowers in a national park.

Toward the end of the third week, I summed up my honeymoon in this letter to Mamma:

New York
1959

Dearest Mamma,

I am still in love—even more than ever. Steven is being very thoughtful. He has dried dishes now for three weeks. He has loved this place since boyhood. It has beautiful scenery—but that is all I can say for it. I can see why Steven felt so at home in Norway if this type of setting pleases him.

I know I have gotten a good husband. I hope I can do my best to make life easier for him. It appears that being born a Rockefeller has made many problems for him, the kind that I have been spared. I can see how the name Rasmussen is much easier to carry.

It will take me some time to fully accept or understand everyone's way of acting and speaking. Certain new ideas and things get to me, to say nothing of my nervous system. I am not unhappy—only tired of learning at all times.

Did you know that the United States has many national parks and that Steven's grandfather created and was responsible for: the Acadia in Maine, the Shenandoah in the Blue Ridge Mountains of Virginia, the Great Smoky Mountains, and the Grand Teton National Park, here where I am staying. I have learned quickly about national parks.

I have also learned to ride a horse. You should see how much I

look a part of the Wild West. Steven even put my hair in a ponytail.
I look terrible.
  Could you possibly send my winter clothes to 810 Fifth Avenue?
I am upset to have forgotten them.

                              Much love,
                              Your Mia

When our honeymoon was over we traveled back to New York, alternately staying at 810 Fifth Avenue and Pocantico until we found our own apartment.

Winthrop, Jr., who was at Pocantico visiting his father, was the first of all the Rockefeller children to come and greet me on our arrival at the estate. He ran from the cutting garden—there were formal gardens, greenhouses, and a garden just for picking—with a handful of flowers of every imaginable color. Bobo Rockefeller passed through my mind, and I decided she must be a good mother to have such a thoughtful and outgoing son, sensitive to flowers and new brides.

Steven's mother was warm and welcoming. I had spent a great deal of time on the estate as a maid and as Steven's secret date. How strange and how different it felt to be there as a member of the family!

The first Rockefeller function we attended was a luncheon that John D. Rockefeller, Jr., gave for Steven and me at Kykuit. I asked Steven what I might wear to such an occasion, and he suggested my native Norwegian costume. When we arrived, his grandfather was sitting in a wheel chair by the living-room window. I went right to him to shake his hand, and he kissed me on both cheeks. His wife was by his side and also welcomed me warmly, and my nervousness disappeared.

The conversation at the table had mostly to do with family matters and nostalgic reminiscences about the past. It was clear that the old man was very fond of Steven, and I began to feel very fond of him. I told him how much I enjoyed the lilies of the valley floating in our finger bowls, because they grow wild in Norway, and I had always loved picking them. With shaking fingers, he ever so gently took the spray out of his bowl and placed it in mine. In the way he spoke, with kindness, warmth, and gentleness, he reminded me of *Bestefar.* As we would say in Norway, "He is a *Sunday* person."

> Tarrytown
> September 26, 1959
>
> Dear Mamma, Pappa, and Torhild,
>
> It seems that Steven's sweetness comes from his grandfather. Before my next visit to him I hope I remember to take an extra dosage of vitamins to help with all the energy loss.
>
> Mr. Rockefeller's house is not to be believed—guess not even in the movies would you see anything like it.
>
> Lunch lasted from one to two P.M.
>
> His kiss on the cheek felt good and gave me a warm and wholesome feeling. He is now eighty-seven years old. I was touched at his prayer before the meal. Everything and everybody was quiet in the true sense of the word.
>
> Mr. Rockefeller gave a feeling of holiness—I can't describe him more—that word tells everything about my feelings for him.
>
> Love,
> Mia

Between all our greetings and meetings with the various members of the family, Steven began to look for an apartment and I concerned myself with the task of writing thank-you notes, which was still overwhelming even though I had already sent more than seven hundred.

One day Steven came home very upset. His real-estate agent, who happened to be Jewish, had told him about a lovely apartment building with "distinctive clientele," meaning no Jews were accepted. Steven dropped the anti-Semitic Jewish agent. He told me about his activities, during senior year at Princeton, as chairman of the committee that co-ordinated the selection of sophomores for the social and eating clubs. I began to understand how much sensitivity, political awareness, and wisdom it had taken to accomplish an almost impossible result. "Bicker" that year was to be "100 per cent," which meant finding a place for Jewish students, too, in the previously exclusive clubs. (The acceptance of blacks and women hadn't even begun to surface as a problem.) The publicity he received then for his personal strength, his lack of bias, and his sense of justice made him seem a likely candidate to follow in his father's footsteps as a national leader.

> *Tarrytown*
> *October 2, 1959*

Dear Mamma,

Things are going well with Steven and me, but I can see we have a long road ahead, full of twists and turns. I am worrying about the purchase of an apartment. They all seem too expensive, although I keep getting dollars and kroner mixed up. Steven laughs when he says he will find a place with a nice sunny room for Steven, Jr. Steven, Jr.—can you imagine!?

I have written, by hand, thirty-three thank-you letters today. Would like to throw myself in bed on a soft pillow and dream of good and peaceful days (even though I didn't always think they were good and peaceful at the time). Guess it is all a state of mind.

The reporters are not leaving us alone. Why don't they find someone else to write about? I am getting tired of reading about us.

I play and sing for hours on my zither. Steven should only know that almost all my songs are religious. He sits and seems to enjoy them so much. I better start to study more in books. Steven understands so much, I would like to understand more, too.

> *Love,*
> *Mia*

> *Tarrytown*
> *October 10, 1959*

Dear Mamma,

Tonight I had a complicated conversation with Steven about religion. Perhaps at a later date I may be able to understand him

*better. Tonight I wanted to be excused from the room—to clean
drawers or anything else to avoid the discussion.*

*I have also gone to church with Steven, but even the minister and
his sermon were different than in Norway.*

*My life has become much more easy on certain grounds, but
much more difficult on others.*

Hope you understand.

Love,
Mia

I could see that religion had the potential of bringing us
closer together. Perhaps if we could share one thing that
meant the same to both of us, other things would follow.
When I read in the paper that "Norway's Billy Graham,"
John Olav Larsen, was speaking at the church in Brooklyn, I
did everything I could to persuade Steven to take me to hear
him. Reluctantly he agreed.

His car had broken down, so we had to borrow Mrs.
Rockefeller's Rolls-Royce. The meeting was conducted in
Norwegian, but one didn't have to understand the language
to know when it was time for members of the audience to
come to the altar to profess their faith and be "saved." The
whole evening made Steven uneasy, even when we were
invited to have coffee in the church basement afterward.
When we left, we discovered the Rolls-Royce stuck between
two other parked cars. People started to crowd around us,
and Steven said (quite seriously!) that someone might think
we had stolen the car and call the police. I thought that was
ridiculous, but by the time he got the Rolls-Royce free he
was really upset, and that made me feel tense, too.

On the way home Steven expressed his doubt about the
value of the "preaching and saving" done by that kind of
evangelist. He said even with the thousands of converts Billy
Graham made in this country, the churches didn't show any
rise in membership, not did the conversions make any
significant change in Christian attitudes. He also felt that

people's emotions were manipulated, wrongly, by the sentimental music and the drama of revival meetings, and not by real religious convictions.

I thought back to other times I had gone to the church in Brooklyn, while I was working for the Rockefellers and dating Steven. After the service I would pass the Sons of Norway dance hall on Eighth Avenue on my way to the subway back home. Often I would go in to dance—I couldn't resist—but immediately I felt like a sinner. Once I called Steven at Princeton to tell him about my constant dilemma: choosing between good and evil, between the love I had for Jesus Christ and the type of physical feelings I had for Steven. He tried to explain to me then that my concept of religion was not profound, that the religion taught me in Norway had been an emotional conditioning process that had filled me with fears that would hamper my growth as a mature woman. He seemed to understand me, because he said he was trying to free himself of a way of life that had placed as many burdens on him as my religion had on me.

Now here I was married, and still feeling I had to choose. Profound? I didn't even know what the word meant. I wasn't capable of thinking abstractly, so I concluded that anything I didn't understand must be profound—even the meaning of "budget."

One evening we had a discussion of the serious responsibility of handling money. Steven told me he had found a suitable apartment and we would be moving as soon as it was cleaned and painted. He asked me how much money I would need in a month for my own personal use. If I could tell him an approximate amount, he would set up a checking account and give me a monthly allowance. He tried to explain about our household expenses and what a budget meant, but I didn't want to listen, I didn't want to deal with such complicated matters, and most of all I didn't want Steven to make this type of confusing demand on me.

All I wanted was love and sympathy—to be pampered and to hear Steven say, just as Pappa and *Bestefar* always had, "I understand you, Mia."

Since I couldn't come up with an amount, Steven suggested, to start with, two hundred fifty dollars a month for my personal use. He also volunteered to go with me to pick out a couple of cocktail dresses at Bergdorf's. (One was gold brocade, with satin trim, and the other purple, a fine French crepe.) However, he told me this would be the last time he could shop with me; I had to learn to do this on my own, and develop my own taste. (I've had those two dresses remade many times according to the latest fashion, and I'll probably go on doing so until I'm a grandmother or the material wears out.)

Another "profundity" was decorum. I loved hugging and kissing Steven at all times and in all places. At first he was very patient and tried to make me understand that among well-bred people there was a right time and place for affection. This new declaration made me nervous. Why, now that we were married, couldn't I hug him anytime I pleased? I began to get butterflies in my stomach whenever I was with him. His sensitive but careful and controlled way of behaving made me feel like a lovesick girl, in need of constant physical attention. Even when it was forthcoming, it didn't seem enough—just like my portions of food at the Rockefeller dinners!

This attitude of Steven's confused me. It seemed as though he had one foot in the Rockefeller world and one in the natural world I represented. But if I acted "naturally" he would retreat to his formal side, which reinforced my childish need to be uncontrolled and spontaneous.

When Steven started to work full time for the president of Rockefeller Center as a junior executive, I had a rude awakening. I now see that on some level I had really expected that his full-time occupation would be to love and take care of me. I had really believed the fairy-tale promise that I would live "happily ever after."

Childishly and unrealistically, I felt rejected. I began to alternate between tears, sobs, pouting, and anger, and letters and notes filled with pleas for forgiveness. Steven would just say, "That's all right, Mia, we'll do better next time," or "You better do some thinking about your behavior." Often, when I was upset, I liked to listen to music, and in the first five years of our marriage I completely wore out two records of Tchaikovsky's Piano Concerto No. 1, with Van Cliburn as soloist and Kiril Kondrashin conducting. This particular record was especially effective at triggering my tears. Steven became adept at turning off the record player as I sat sobbing for some reason unknown to us both.

How upsetting it must have been for him to witness such outbursts of emotion in his bride, who had managed to hide all her tears before the marriage. Perhaps Mamma's longings and emotional pattern had caught up with me. I became frightened when Steven mentioned that the possibility had occurred to him too. What a worry to think that sadness was an integral part of my personality, that I would carry my island melancholia with me, always feeling damp and cold inside. The only time I felt secure was when Steven was talking to, teaching, or focusing directly on me, without even a dog in the room to distract him. My moods became as erratic as the weather on Borøya.

One day, while we were still staying at 810 Fifth Avenue, I received a telegram from Pappa:

PLEASE MEET ME IN CANADA. YOUR PAPPA.

At a time when I needed Pappa most, I resented his coming. Although Steven's parents had many guest rooms, I felt embarrassed because my father was arriving unannounced, and because he thought Canada was right next door to New York. I couldn't drive, so I had to ask Uncle Andres to pick him up.

Pappa got to Canada by signing on as a member of the crew on a Norwegian freighter, *Sunpolyna*. Actually, he didn't have to work; he had merely used this ploy to avoid any publicity about "taking Nelson up on his offer to come to America for a visit."

When he arrived I told him he really should have waited until we were in our own home, but we would have a good time anyway. In fact, the Rockefellers thought it was great that my father cared enough to come all the way to New York to check up on me after such a short time. He explained that my letters were not enough, and he wanted to see this new world of mine for himself. I felt I couldn't leave him alone with anyone because he didn't understand English, but he didn't seem aware of my discomfort. He had nothing but warm and good feelings about the Rockefellers and all he saw and did with them, and he begged me to take advantage of the great opportunities offered to me, especially in education. Noting how large and impersonal New York was, he suggested I make a few good friends, to give me a feeling of belonging.

"What is this world without friends?" he demanded.

When I took him to the airport after two weeks, he said, "Be good to your family here. Do the best in whatever you may be doing. If you need help, you know where I am. Whatever happens to you, remember that you will always have your father's strong love and belief in you."

I felt a little guilty, but I told him that the next time he came to New York he should bring my mother along, and it should *not* be a surprise visit. I was leading a different kind of life now, and visits always needed to be planned in advance. But Steven had found Pappa's visit thoroughly delightful and amusing.

Tarrytown
November 8, 1959

Dear Mamma,

I am happy in spite of "knots on the thread" at times. Can't wait to move into our first home. I am going to take good care of Steven, alone, and without my salary as a maid!

Tomorrow he is going to buy me a cat, since I do not have enough live things to care for. I need someone or something close to me at all times, it seems. Steven is sitting in his wing-back chair that he has just recently had reupholstered. He found it discarded on the estate, about to be given to the Salvation Army. He is very proud of saving it. He looks at peace with the world. Isn't he lucky? What is his secret? Good night and sleep soundly, everyone!

Hearty Greetings,
Your Mia

Tarrytown
November 24, 1959

Dear Pappa,

Tomorrow night we are moving into 150 East 73rd Street. Wedding presents are still coming. Last weekend Mr. and Mrs. Rockefeller had a party in our honor. Almost everyone was unknown to me, and strange in different ways if not in name.

I have bought myself two canaries—a little song in the morning is good for all of us. Wish you could bring Mamma here for a visit—yes, perhaps it could be the honeymoon you never had. It would be about time you knew such a thing does exist.

Heartily yours,
Mia

Our apartment was lovely. To be a housewife, at last, and to move into something beautiful and *ours* was exciting for me, and I forgot about the spiritual doldrums of the past months. Steven and I worked hard together cleaning and fixing, but we painted only a few kitchen cabinets—that was enough. Then Steven called in some painters who worked regularly at Rockefeller Center to finish the entire job.

We didn't have a great deal in the way of furniture to arrange—not much more than our bed, and a kitchen table and chairs. We didn't even have a television set. But there were enough paintings and other art objects to decorate every room. Steven was very knowledgeable about the fine art of hanging pictures, so I left that matter to him. My only request was that he place a nude etching by Picasso where I and our future guests couldn't see it. (The picture eventually wound up in *his* bathroom in Tarrytown.)

Every day I used to hang out of the dining-room window, patiently waiting for my husband to come home to me and the meal I had prepared for him. He praised me for my cooking, house cleaning, dishwashing, flower arranging, and the cozy look of the apartment. I felt Norwegian women were taken for granted back home because these things were done automatically by all housewives, rich or poor. Steven was certainly easy to please in the domestic department!

New York
December 3, 1959

Dear Mamma,

Trying to keep Steven happy in our new home, but feel so sick. Could I be pregnant? Please do not mention this to anyone. So, get ready in your mind to be a grandmother. Something is changing in my body.

After each meal I get a great big hug from Steven. Guess I better keep on with the cooking. His hugs feel better to me than food right now.

Love,
Mia

P.S. TOP SECRET

Christmas was coming, and I went to Bloomingdale's to do a little shopping. I purchased a few items, and to my embarrassment had to ask the salesgirl, a former co-worker, for assistance in writing out my first check. I soon found there were other problems about writing checks: either I didn't have any means of identification, like a driver's license, or people didn't believe a check signed "Rockefeller" was anything but a joke, especially considering my accent and behavior. I decided to do as much of my shopping as I could at Bloomingdale's, where some of the salespeople knew me.

But I hadn't written very many checks before Steven received a phone call from the branch of Chase Manhattan Bank at Rockefeller Center, requesting that I use a uniform signature so they could identify and process my checks without any doubts or confusions. I had been changing my handwriting depending on my mood; sometimes I wrote a delicate and fancy script, sometimes a bold one, sometimes I liked to make the letters slope *backward*!

The first formal dance we attended together was the American-Scandinavian Foundation Ball at the Hotel Pierre, on Fifth Avenue. How different this was from the Fireman's Ball in Seal Harbor. The tickets were twenty-five dollars a couple instead of one dollar, important Scandinavian people made important-sounding speeches, and everyone was formally dressed.

When I was introduced to the American-Scandinavian band leader, I had to smile inwardly because we recognized each other from less-fancy Norwegian dances in Brooklyn. We both put on a good act, pretending this was our first meeting, and I was most grateful. In those early days of our marriage I was still unsure of myself and of the way people would receive me.

Steven had an especially good time. He pointed out many women who he thought looked attractive. To me, they were the plainest ones there—they wore little if any make-up, and some had hair that was long, unset, or twisted around the head in what we call lovebraids or *kjaerlighetsfletter.*

The following day Steven came home from the office with

a present for me. It was a long-playing record of Sibelius' *Finlandia*, and on the cover was a girl walking through some pine woods alone, eyes downcast. She was pretty in a simple way and wore her hair in lovebraids. I wondered if Steven had bought the record because of the music or because he wanted me to look like the girl on the cover. I guess I could have asked him, but I was afraid he would say yes. I wanted to look fashionable, not like someone who had just emerged from a walk in the woods.

One day I was listening to the news on the radio, and heard the announcer say that the Governor's daughter-in-law, Mrs. Steven Rockefeller, was expecting a baby. How could that man know for sure when I myself didn't? Had I looked pregnant at the ball? Or maybe some Americans took for granted that Steven had had to marry me. In tears, I called him at his office. He calmly told me not to worry. Most babies take nine months before they are born, and by the time I had mine the period elapsed would be more than enough to reassure everyone. He was right, of course, but the thought of so many people, both here and in Norway, counting on their fingers bothered me.

New York
December 29, 1959

Dear Mamma, Pappa, and Torhild,

Thank you for your perfect Christmas presents. Remember, it is not the most expensive or largest gifts that are most appreciated in life.

Let me tell you how Steven and I spent our first Christmas together:

We celebrated Christmas Eve with Mr. and Mrs. Rockefeller at 810 Fifth Avenue. I was greeted by Mrs. Rockefeller at the elevator with a hug and a kiss. Michael and I did most of the tree decorations. Mr. Rockefeller thought we should open a few pre-Christmas gifts. I received some fancy and rich-looking jewelry from the Governor. Steven told me his father chooses all the gifts he gives by himself. I wonder how Steven, Michael, and Rodman feel when their father gives every one of the ladies such unbelievable gifts.

Steven gave me a two-strand pearl necklace, a scarf, ice figure skates, and many good hugs. I liked the hugs best of all. I will not be able to try any skating this winter. My figure isn't right for my skates.

Christmas Day we went to the annual family dinner at the River Club, a private ladies' club near the East River, as guests of Mr. Rockefeller's only sister, Mrs. Mauzé. Thirty-two family members were present.

I only wish I didn't feel so sick.

Steven loves bringing friends and family to our home to taste Norwegian cooking and holiday baking.

We are still cleaning dishes together.

> *Hearty greetings,*
> *Anne-Marie*

> *New York*
> *January 1960*

Dear Mamma,

Steven is talking about coming to Norway next Christmas with a new member in the family.

I went shopping today and ended up buying a few things you might use. I seem to have too much, too soon—material things, that is.

Steven always studies. He encourages me to find some interests. I do not know what to pursue, because I am told that in this family all roads are open to me.

Must say good night. Steven likes me to go to sleep at the same time he does even though I am sometimes not tired. The lights will be turned off soon.

> *Good night!*
> *Anne-Marie*

The only household chore that didn't thrill me was the laundry, so I hired a laundress to come once a week. It was a pleasure just checking on the starched shirt collars and the neatly ironed sheets and pillowcases. Ida Finne was a hard and conscientious Finnish worker who had previously been employed by Dag Hammarskjöld and by Dwight Eisenhower when he was president of Columbia University. I was proud to have someone so capable looking after our clothing. Yet to Steven, the knife-sharp creases and the clean starchy smells produced by a laundress didn't seem important or impressive.

Steven had a bad habit of leaving his dirty socks lying anywhere in the bathroom that he happened to take them off. I was annoyed at his messiness and told him that I had been his maid once but wouldn't be again—that I distinguished between picking up after him and taking care of the apartment in general. I asked for a maid to help keep the dirty laundry off the floor, but that must have seemed like a too-expensive way of remedying a habit that could be taken care of more easily. He asked me to buy him a cheap wicker hamper at a nearby Japanese store.

My days in the apartment were sometimes long. Not many young people lived in the building, and the few that did were very formal. No one spoke to me, even in the elevator. I had to find something interesting and constructive to do, and with Steven's approval and encouragement I decided to take a course in English at Columbia University.

The registration and the trip to the bursar's office proved to be more difficult than the actual course. I stood in a long line with my pocketbook in hand, waiting interminably to pay the fee. I kept reading over the registration form, and finally I asked the nice-looking girl in front of me if my husband's name should go beside the word "guardian." While we waited together for at least an hour, my newly found friend, Naomi Cohen, helped me go over the entire application. Finally it was Naomi's turn to pay her tuition, and she was twenty-five dollars short. I could see an advantage in having a checking account that day as I quickly wrote out the amount for her.

After we were both through, she invited me downtown to meet her parents and have lunch, and so she could return the borrowed money. The afternoon was so pleasant and went so fast that I almost forgot it was the day for me to have my physical to determine if I was pregnant or not. Just as I was about to leave, I realized I didn't have a slip on. My modesty threw me into a minor panic. Reluctantly, I told Naomi my problem, and without saying anything she quickly produced a pretty, lacy half slip, fancier than anything I owned. It was a small but shared intimacy. I shook her hand and was taken aback when she squeezed my hand with just as much force. I told her she was the strongest woman I had met in America.

I was going to enjoy Naomi's company very much. She worked in her father's bookshop, and her intelligence, sense of humor, and independence impressed me. At her suggestion we both signed up for some volunteer work in the children's ward at Bellevue Hospital. The experience was good for me, and the once-a-week diversion from myself and my small world helped. Naomi would often come by for a Norwegian supper before we went to the hospital. Everyone else seemed pleased at how well I was adjusting.

I met Mrs. Rockefeller, who was going to accompany me to the doctor's office, at her apartment. I told her about Naomi, mentioning she'd confessed to me that she did not like to cook. Thereupon Mrs. Rockefeller also confessed that she could not cook, never had to, and had no interest whatsoever in finding out how. It seemed impossible to me that there were women who couldn't perform this basic domestic function. Admitting it seemed the epitome of helplessness, and I wondered what Mrs. Rockefeller would do if her cooks all quit.

I had never had this kind of examination before, so Mrs. Rockefeller sat by me and asked the doctor all the necessary questions. I was horrified when he said that if a rabbit died, it would establish that I was pregnant. The next day I was told the test was positive.

> New York
> February 6, 1960

Dear Mamma,

Just finished mending six pairs of Steven's socks. Since I've been to the doctor and have been told I am pregnant for sure, it has been reported in all of the papers. Why are people so curious over all of this?

Steven is sleeping in the chair. He even looks like he had a good dinner.

I am starting a course at the Red Cross in the care of babies. It was suggested to me by Mrs. Rockefeller. Can you see me playing with dolls again?

We are twenty pregnant women in the course. Have you ever been in one room with that many women who were expecting a baby? It's very upsetting to me. Thank heavens I'm the smallest one there, at least for the time being. This is not my idea of a useful course, nor is it interesting. I will fail for sure.

> *Hearty greetings,*
> *Mia*

I received a worried call from Mamma that Pappa had suddenly been taken ill. I didn't know how serious his condition was, and decided to go to Norway to find out for myself. Steven couldn't accompany me, but he suggested I travel under the assumed name of Mrs. Clark. This was a mistake, because I was paged at the London airport, didn't recognize my temporary name, missed my connection, and spent a whole day in the airport waiting for another flight.

By the time I arrived home it turned out that Pappa's condition was not at all grave. In fact, he had almost recovered, and after five days I wanted to be back in New York with Steven. But while I was at home I began to think about my sister, Torhild, in a new light. She is naturally more retiring than I, and in the excitement and hubbub of the past year she had been out of my thoughts most of the time. She seemed more at peace with herself, even though she didn't much care about changing fashions, or men, or social life.

I invited her to come back to New York with me to stay with Steven and me and study English at Columbia University. I wanted to do something for her, and I also felt she could help me with the new baby. The fact that she had a personality like a pool of serenity crossed my mind, too. Perhaps she could calm the stormy sea that was brewing inside me and the marriage as well.

Although we both carried Norway with us to America, New York affected my sister in a completely different way than it had me. She could not stand the pace, the pressure, or the noise of traffic. And she remarked to me soon after her arrival that all the comforts and fame I had acquired would not necessarily make me happy.

I introduced Torhild to a Norwegian man whom I had met when I first came to this country. Torhild told him, "If you like Anne-Marie in any way, you will not care for me." He responded by admitting he had never gotten to know me because I always had too many boy friends for his liking. He remembered going to church in Brooklyn with me and meeting two other men with whom I had also planned to go to church, but had forgotten about. All four of us sat together, and it was too much for him. Torhild proved to be exactly the type of girl he was looking for, and the two fell quietly and secretly in love. But this turned out to be a very brief romance, and it ended tragically. One weekend Torhild went to see Niagara Falls with her Norwegian-American English teacher, and while she was away he was murdered in Harlem. We both attended the funeral and tried to be as helpful as we could to the young man's family. After the funeral, his father gave Torhild a gold ring etched with small stars. It was only then that I realized the depth of feeling between the two.

Torhild already had her driver's license, and she would take me around on weekends in Tarrytown. Soon I started to practice in our old convertible, too. One day I took my part-time summer cook, Louise, out for a drive. The guard at the main gate looked surprised, but he didn't say anything, and I drove on, out to the public road. It was really crazy. I didn't know how to use the blinkers or switch on the lights, or how to go into reverse. The cook prayed out loud the whole time I was driving around. I did have sense enough to stay on quiet back roads, and somehow we made it back to the estate safely, but then I lost control and drove the dilapidated Ford onto the golf course that was next to Kykuit. The gardener and the mechanic helped me out of that scrape.

I decided to take proper driving lessons, and in 1963 I finally got a license. My reputation as a driver didn't improve, however. I was stopped for speeding seven times in one year. Once I talked my way out of a ticket by telling the policeman I had a stingy husband who wouldn't allow me to hire a chauffeur. I was warned that the policemen on the parkway knew my car, so I should drive more carefully for my own good. Steven eventually bought me a Mustang, and I'm afraid I drove it aggressively fast, especially in times of frustration.

In addition to learning how to drive, bowl, swim, ride a horse, speak better English, and have a baby according to the Red Cross, I also studied, religiously, a book called *Etiquette*, by Emily Post. Just as I was beginning to feel prepared to deal correctly with any event that came up in the Rockefeller family I was taken by surprise by the death of Steven's

ry Rockefeller and Anne-Marie with Stevie

Nelson and Steven with Stevie

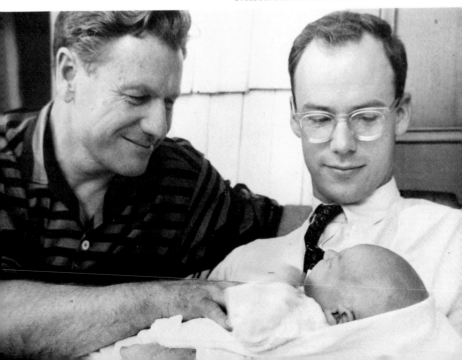

ABOVE:
Anne-Marie,
her parents, and her
Svendsen grandparents
with Stevie,
Norway, 1961

RIGHT:
Steven with Ingrid
and Jennifer, 1967

After Jennifer's baptism, summer 1965:
Stevie, Jennifer, and Ingrid with Anne-Marie

Steven in Rockefeller Center, fall 1959
Alfred Eisenstadt, Time/Life Picture Agency

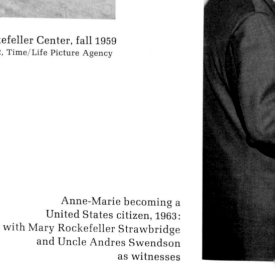

Anne-Marie becoming a
United States citizen, 1963:
with Mary Rockefeller Strawbridge
and Uncle Andres Swendson
as witnesses

The living room and dining room of Ormelia, Søgne, 1967

Ann Rockefeller
Pierson and Anne-Marie
in Scandinavians for
Rockefeller headquarters, 1968

Conrad Waldinger

Anne-Marie and Steven
at the Pocantico Hills
reception

ne-Marie and Nelson at the Norwegian's Children's Home in Brooklyn

ne-Marie in her apartment with Dr. Alexander Winogradow, 1967

Bradshaw Mintener, Jr.

Visiting the Head Start progra
at Bethel Lutheran Churc
Madison, Wisconsin

Anne-Marie and Torhild
in Norwegian costume, 1971

grandfather. Mrs. Post had no helpful hints on how to mourn with grace and dignity.

Everyone in the family bore his or her grief with reserve. I did fairly well myself until the Memorial Service at Riverside Church, which had been built by Steven's grandfather, where I went completely to pieces when I heard the familiar and moving song "Goin' Home," adapted from Dvorak's New World Symphony, played by two serious-looking violinists, one white and one black. I cried hard, and since nobody else was crying at all I was terribly conspicuous. I felt ashamed as Steven and Mrs. Rockefeller escorted me out a side entrance, and hoped the rest of the family would think it was my pregnancy that had made me so sensitive and emotional.

But in a way I was even more upset when the family assembled for the burial service. The Rockefellers have a private cemetery outside the fenced estate property. It is small, secluded, and completely contained within its own set of gates and fences. And a new sadness crept into my consciousness during that brief service: even in death, I thought, this family was isolated from the rest of the world, where no friends could come at will to visit, place flowers, or say a prayer.

I asked Steven why his grandfather had merely been made into some ashes in an urn, why there hadn't been a viewing, and other questions that to him seemed pointless or impolite. I learned more about the death of John D. Rockefeller, Jr., from the newspapers than I did from the Rockefeller family.

Maybe it seems macabre, but back in the district where I come from all aspects of a death are discussed. It is a way of showing compassion and consideration, and it is a relief from the sorrow felt by the mourners. The body of the loved one is bathed, and dressed all in white. It is then allowed to lie in a cool room for some days, while friends come to weep, talk, and accept this particular death as a reality in their lives. Graves are a part of the living. They are planted with flowers and shrubs, and watered faithfully by members of the family. Graveyards most certainly are not walled off, but are open to all, lying within the shadow and view of the church.

How different and shocking this death was for me. I never quite understood the different system until years later when I read Nancy Mitford's *The American Way of Death*, which answered the questions Steven and I had never discussed. With fascination I read, in detail, how the blood is removed from the veins, embalming fluid injected, and other devices and embellishments added to make the deceased look alive and beautiful. This thoroughly frightened me—so much so that I saw a lawyer and had three pages added to my will concerning how I was to be treated after my death. It was an unusual request for the lawyer, but he followed the orders: no American funeral for me. Not that I felt death was close at hand. I just wanted my friends to feel free to cry and grieve as loudly as they pleased, and to be able to recognize me as I had lived.

Before old Mr. Rockefeller's death, we had been given a Victorian frame house on the estate to use on the weekends and holidays. The house had always been called the Stevens House. I never did find out why; it was just a coincidence that Steven and I lived in it for a time. Over the years many members of the Rockefeller family had used this house until they acquired one of their own. Bobo and Winthrop Rockefeller lived there before their divorce, and Roddy and Barbara were the tenants ahead of us.

The house was old and roomy. The kitchen had an antique stove, icebox, and sink. The counters were orange, and the wallpaper was a mass of large ugly tulips, each of them at least a foot tall. The bathrooms were equally antiquated. The toilets were actually water closets, with tanks overhead, and the water was released by a hard tug on a chain. The wallpaper in each room was dark and dingy and looked to me as if it hadn't been changed in a hundred years. I couldn't understand why none of the other Rockefellers had bothered to fix it up more. Steven couldn't understand why I didn't accept the charm of things as they were. He also didn't want me to say too much about the house, because I might hurt the feelings of those who had lived there comfortably before us.

Steven would often sit on the gingerbread-trimmed porch overlooking the Hudson River for hours when he wasn't reading, and come back into the living room with such a look of peace on his face. There was something in his contentment and Torhild's—so much like Pappa's—that made me feel envious and in awe of them.

When I sat on that porch and looked at the river, I either became romantic, sentimental, and teary, or I felt the whole world was passing me by, just as the river was, and then I would become restless.

Next to the Stevens House was a smaller home that was occupied by the Governor's farmer/caretaker, Mr. Moore, and his wife. Mrs. Moore did not have a washer or dryer, and Steven told me we must share our appliances with her. I was slightly uncomfortable every time she brought her laundry over. Her discussions didn't interest me in the least, and I felt she would have preferred the house to remain vacant. I don't think the Moores ever got used to my not being a maid any more. Of all the help on the estate, they were the only ones who found it uncomfortable to call me Mrs. Steven. If they called me anything, it was Anne-Marie. I suspected Steven of having the fantasy that we were just a simple young couple living next door to a farmer whose wife came over to borrow sugar and exchange recipes, especially for brownies and oatmeal cookies.

New York
March 1960

Dear Mamma and Pappa,

I talked to my doctor today and told him I wanted to have my baby at home—just like the women do on Borøya. He does not think this would be wise. He tells me it is different here—everyone has her baby in a hospital, for safety's sake. I would not want to jeopardize my baby's life, so I will go to the hospital even though I love my home and would be happier here. The doctor promises me I will be as comfortable as he can make it for me.

I have received many letters from strangers telling me I will have a boy. I am beginning to think so, too. He kicks so hard. Maybe he will be a soccer player like his Daddy was at Princeton.

The doctor is too serious and businesslike for my taste. He doesn't seem to have any time for listening to me about my discomforts.

Steven went to talk to the doctor, too, about the delivery. He likes to be prepared for and study everything.

IMPORTANT: Pappa—Steven is Mr., Mia is Mrs., and Torhild is Miss. Can't you try to learn that much English, please?

Love,
Mia

As it turned out, I received my advice about childbirth from a black woman who was supervising the children's riding at the stables. I asked her what it was really like to have a baby, thinking she would know because she had told me she had six children. She said, "Ma'am, it hurts . . . it is really bad. I have to admit the first one was the worst, but the others were not much better. But I have to say it was worth it."

In March, Mr. and Mrs. Rockefeller took Mary and me to another one of their homes, Hacienda Montesacro, in Venezuela. In some ways I was sad to leave Steven, and I put twelve red roses by his bedside, but I felt good about going on a trip with his parents, as though I were a daughter and not just a daughter-in-law.

The house in Venezuela was beautiful and fully staffed with hard-working people. I shared a bedroom with Mary, and we sat up most of the night chattering like two schoolgirls. I talked her into sneaking to the refrigerator for a late-night snack, but the sight of some cockroaches abated our hunger.

When we got back to our room, we looked out the window at a sky that was lighted up to a bright orange color by something burning fiercely. Frightened that we were all going to turn to ashes, I told Mary to run for her father, even if it was the middle of the night, because it must be the end of the world, just as it is described in the Bible. If the Governor minded being waked up, or thought the doomsday prophet sharing his daughter's room was funny, he didn't show it. He was very reassuring, and told us the sky was orange because the natives were burning the fields to make them fertile.

The next day he took us for a drive to prove it. It was interesting to see the difference between South American ranches and Western ones. Mr. Rockefeller also took me on a tour of a coffee plantation. I really enjoyed that brief stay in Venezuela, and I think I'm glad, now, that I had no way of knowing it would be the last trip the Governor and Mrs. Rockefeller would take there as man and wife.

New York
May 27, 1960

Dear Mamma and Pappa,
This weekend I received some house plants from Mrs. Rockefeller as a gift. I think she has to take them back to her greenhouse. I can't seem to get anything to grow here.

We hardly ever go out. Guess we will grow old before our time. I can't understand this unexpected quiet life. Our apartment is kept in order, each corner and each shelf waiting for someone—any-one—to come and inspect. Yes, even you, Mamma, because you care about such matters. Not many others do.

My girl friend Naomi is coming tonight. She is a good friend and interesting to be with in all this quietness. She gives me a different outlook on life.

Glad to have a roof over my head. The rain is coming down harder than I have ever seen. Through the rain and the fog I can see millions of lights twinkling in the city. I wonder what everyone is doing behind those lighted windows?

Please use air mail paper and envelopes. The postage will be cheaper—maybe I would receive more letters from you more often.

Love,
Anne-Marie

Tarrytown
June 4, 1960

Dear Mamma and Pappa,

It is raining and there is lots of thunder. Mary's dog Sonny is here at my feet. We are the only ones not enjoying the day. I can still remember hiding in the woodshed when we had such weather as this on Borøya. Pappa, remember how I would put on your big rubber boots for extra safety? I believe it was you, Mamma, who showed us how to be so careful and rightfully afraid. No one worries about thunder here.

I am now listening to some sentimental Norwegian songs. Steven tries to tolerate them "these days" to make me feel at home.

He is wondering what to buy for me when the baby is born. I did not know I would receive a present for having a baby. I learn something new every day.

I am taking more English lessons from Mr. Long, who was one of Steven's teachers when he was a little boy at the Buckley School for Boys in New York City. He told me Steven was his favorite pupil, very bright and well behaved in every way, and I am a lucky girl to be married to him. Everyone tells me I am lucky! I think Steven is looking forward to having a child—one he hopes he will be able to train to stand still in the woods while studying and appreciating the sounds of nature, especially wild birds. I do not have enough patience or interest in his feathered friends. I regret my lack of enthusiasm.

Love,
Mia

I knew Steven had a deep respect and love for nature, and was especially interested in birds, but I hadn't realized how intense that interest was. I felt very selfish during some of our nature walks, when I wished to be the one admired and watched. I used to like the sea gulls and songbirds, but watching Steven make a science out of the color, sex, and migration pattern of birds was turning me into a bird hater. He even spoke of joining a professional bird watchers' club in Central Park, but I was able to persuade him not to. To make a professional hobby of watching birds seemed ridiculous and boring to me, in those weeks while I was waiting for our baby to be born.

One day, when I was in one of my "jealous-of-the-birds" moods, I thought of a good trick to play on Steven. I had bought a few beautifully stuffed rare birds in vibrant colors, and one day, while Steven was busy in his study, I carefully arranged them on the branches of a bush that was directly in view of his place at the dining-room table. I waited until we were partway through lunch, and then I said: "Look, Guggen! Look at those birds outside. What kind are they?"

Steven was startled, first by my interest in birds and then by the phenomenon before him. He did not usually wear his glasses at mealtimes, but he found them in a hurry and rushed outside to investigate. The expensive joke was on me when I saw the disappointment on his face and realized how sad it was to be jealous of a few birds and the attention they received. Thank goodness we both ended up laughing, that time.

I had taken to calling him Guggen. I would often hear the Rockefellers and other sophisticated people call each other "sweetie" and "darling," but I couldn't bring myself to use these terms of endearment. We don't say them in Norway. A cup of coffee or a gesture takes the place of, and means more than, all the sweet words. Nevertheless, there was something appealing about the gushy words—almost like the sound a baby makes when cooing and wooing his parents. One day, when I was in a particularly cuddly mood, out came the word "Guggen." Later, Steven said if he was Guggen then I must be Guggi. I treasured those two words because they conjured up an image in my mind of how I wanted to feel as Steven's wife—dependent, cuddly, lovey-dovey. I can never figure out why he didn't mind our using those terms for each other in public—maybe he believed everyone thought they meant something else in Norwegian.

Tarrytown
July 13, 1960

Dear Mamma and Pappa,

Steven has taken off from work the last weeks to be with me before the baby arrives. He is getting nervous being home with me and just waiting. So am I. I told him to please go back to the office. I do not have any patience left in waiting for this baby. I want each letter to be the last before the good news—but no luck.

Mrs. Rockefeller keeps telling me to teach her, Mary, and Ann baking and cooking—can you imagine?

The summer heat here is terrible. I am suffering like a dog. (Sonny is here at my feet and looking up at me. I think he understands my feelings on the matter.) There is no air conditioning in any of the homes on the estate, only wishful thinking that a breeze will come across the river.

I gave my plants vitamins. Hope it helps because I want many living things around me.

Hearty greetings,
Anne-Marie

Columbia Presbyterian
Hospital
New York City
July 22, 1960

Dear, dear, Mamma and Pappa,

Our beautiful baby son arrived on July 21—a large, still little, Rasmussen-Rockefeller. It was hard work. He weighed eight pounds and four ounces. I have already walked around the room. Pretty good for ten hours after such an ordeal. I am so happy and proud!!! I hope the name Steven, Jr., meets with his daddy's approval. For some reason Governor Rockefeller didn't want any of his sons named after him. I hope this is not the case with Steven.

I will write more when I am stronger. There has been much excitement—many telegrams, flowers, and presents.

Proudly,
Your Mia

New York
July 28, 1960

Dear Mamma and Pappa,

I came home to our apartment with Steven, Jr., today. He seems so content in his basket in the nursery. Steven and the nurse came to pick us up. We have hired a nurse and a cleaning lady to come once a week. Mrs. Rockefeller helped me with the interviews. She asked all the questions. I felt sorry for Mrs. Conlon, but I was relieved that it was she answering the ad for a job and not I.

Mrs. Conlon is Irish, and slightly superstitious, I think. She told us she didn't want to be responsible for a "Rockefeller" baby if we go to the country on weekends. She believes country rats definitely attack nursing mothers. Mamma, is there any truth in this? Steven had to reassure her there would be no rats at Pocantico Hills Estate.

It feels so good to hold little Stevie as he rests his head on my shoulder. Steven goes around with a beaming smile on his face constantly. He is such a proud new father, but still cannot hold Stevie without some fear. I can't blame him.

I love both Stevens so much. Stevie was three weeks overdue, but all waiting is forgotten now.

The mailman is kept very busy these days. We are getting greetings from all over the world—presents too! How can I write more thank-you letters? The wedding notes have just been completed. I wish I would receive more cards and letters from those I know and love.

Hearty greetings,
Anne-Marie

Mrs. Rockefeller gave me the baby blanket she had been working on from the beginning of my pregnancy. She had carried the white blanket and yarn in a plastic bag with her while she was knitting it. She apologized for not being more gifted at handwork, knowing how skilled my relatives were, but I cherished her gift because I realized how much love and effort she had put into it.

I was also given Steven's first silver knife, fork, pusher, and cup, and many other lovely things he'd had as a baby. I loved mending and starching some of his baby clothing Mrs. Rockefeller gave me, and was pleased to see that she, too, had a sentimental side. The two of us enjoyed each other's company as never before.

I was concerned because Stevie didn't have much hair, but Mrs. Rockefeller assured me that this was quite normal, and predicted that he would soon have a healthy growth all over his head—I just had to be patient. The consensus was that Stevie was indeed a *beautiful* baby.

Stevie's presents from his Granddaddy and Grandmother Rockefeller were two silver hairbrushes (when I didn't understand why two, I was told it was some kind of family tradition) and a silver plate. Mr. Rockefeller personally sent a huge vase filled with orchids of various hues to me at the hospital. It was the most unusual and outstanding floral composition I have ever seen.

In contrast to the extravagant orchids sat Steven's charming and welcome bouquet of "sweetheart roses" in a cute basket. The thoughtful note he sent with it meant more to me than all the flowers and plants in the room.

When Michael came to see his new nephew, he took one look at Stevie and said, "He looks just like Buddha, Chiefy. Congratulations!"

Michael had been with Steven on a family trip to Japan, where Steven had purchased a large Buddha figurine. I guess Michael meant his remark to be the supreme compliment, but *my* beautiful baby bore no resemblance to any religious leader—Christian, Jewish, or Buddhist—and I hoped he never would.

I had been home from the hospital only a short time when Steven announced we were having guests. While I was visiting Pappa in Norway, Steven had gone to Kent, Connecticut, to spend a weekend with Betty and Jack

Sapoch—Jack had been a friend and clubmate of Steven's at Princeton University—and now Steven wanted to return their hospitality.

I didn't welcome the idea of having some "Princeton people" as guests so soon after the birth of my baby. Besides, Betty had sent us a utensil that looked to me like delivery forceps—more cruel American humor, I thought. So for a while after they arrived I wasn't very conversational, though I listened with relief as Betty cleared away my misconception about what were actually asparagus tongs. Apparently Steven had admired a pair on one of his visits to Kent, so Betty sent another pair to us. I became more comfortable as the evening went on, and when Jack told us he was going off on a business trip soon, I impulsively asked Betty to spend the time with me in Pocantico, even though I knew Steven was somewhat hesitant about inviting friends to stay there. He always felt obliged to explain that his great-grandfather and grandfather had built and established the luxurious compound, but that the younger members of the Rockefeller family lived quite modestly, and someday, he believed and hoped, the whole estate would be enjoyed by great numbers of people who were not Rockefellers. He would much rather tell friends about the restored home of Washington Irving in nearby Sleepy Hollow than give them a tour of the estate.

The splendors of Pocantico didn't seem to overwhelm or dazzle Betty. She just told me that everything visible was very beautiful—I had to agree with her—and left it at that. She seemed to enjoy my company, and also my customary exuberance, which was certainly different from her quiet manner! I made her laugh frequently, and what could have been more warming and reassuring?

Once, I told her how difficult I found it was to write thank-you letters. She offered to help, and the suggestions she gave me about formal notes to congressmen, senators, and other political figures made the task much easier for me.

One day we went horseback riding together, and afterward I suggested a drive into town. Betty wanted to change clothes, because she had borrowed Steven's jeans and shirt, and she's just one inch over five feet. I told her we didn't have to look like models just to go outside the gates, and took her to the family garage. "Pick one you can drive," I told her.

That was the one time Betty did seem overwhelmed. Spread out before her, in addition to the regular family cars, was Winthrop Rockefeller's collection of antique cars, including a wooden one. There was also a small, three-wheeled Isetta, with a door that opened in front, belonging to Nelson. She settled on the Isetta, which did look about the right size for her.

She got it started all right, and although the inside door handle and other things began falling off as we went along, we did finally make it into the middle of town. There Betty decided she'd better pull over to the curb, and a policeman promptly came up to give us a ticket. Betty didn't have her driver's license along, but after much frantic searching through the glove compartment I found the registration. The policeman did a double take when he read the card, which proclaimed Governor Rockefeller as the owner of the "vehicle." I had trouble keeping a straight face as I watched him deciding we couldn't have stolen it. But he surely did wonder what the Governor was doing with such a small and junky car, and why he had allowed us on Tarrytown's main street with it. He advised us to get back to the estate fast, before someone else gave us a ticket.

The two of us laughed and giggled like teen-agers as we jerked home in the sputtering Isetta. It felt so good to do something I wasn't allowed to do. We made a pact not to tell Steven about our afternoon's adventures—and I believe nobody has told him to this day.

When Jack came to pick Betty up, we all celebrated their

second wedding anniversary. I wondered how I would feel at the end of two years of marriage to Steven, and if the Sapochs had similar problems—though I must admit it didn't seem likely.

We spent the latter part of the summer in Maine, returning to New York in the middle of September—to learn from the newspapers that my name was now included in the Social Register. I was not much impressed, and neither was Steven, for that matter, though he did explain what the Social Register was.

I did not re-enter Columbia University. The private English tutoring was going well, and I found it more comfortable than going to class, where reporters were still trying to follow me around in order to get a glimpse of my life as a Rockefeller. I did continue my volunteer work at Bellevue Hospital with Naomi.

Steven had decided not to go back to work at Rockefeller Center. He had been searching within himself for some time, and knew by now that he needed to do something that would bring him more answers to his philosophical and metaphysical questions. After much deliberation, he decided to enroll at Union Theological Seminary. He knew his family, especially his father, was counting on him to make some significant personal contribution to the political or philanthropic world. He convinced his father that the combination of a philosophical and religious background would provide him with the insight now missing in most national leaders. The iron strength of Steven's conviction convinced his father that he was following the wisest course. Steven often told me how much of a burden the younger generation of Rockefellers found these high expectations for them, and how much courage it took to follow another path.

Shortly after his studies began I was invited to come to the school to meet his professors and friends. I couldn't believe my ears when I entered the building and heard the students singing "Three Blind Mice." I had expected them to be singing hymns, and I never did find out why they had chosen that childish though gruesome nursery rhyme. But on my second visit I was invited by a group of faculty wives to meet Mrs. Franklin D. Roosevelt, who was to be guest of honor and chief speaker at a luncheon meeting. I had a soft spot in my heart for her. I admired the way she met the challenge of being married to a famous man, and I was also personally grateful to her. When my marriage to Steven was first announced she was the only prominent person in the United States, or anywhere else, as far as I know, who spoke out publicly against news stories stressing the fact that I had been a maid—as if I had been indentured and had worked for the Rockefellers all my life. Mrs. Roosevelt was quoted as saying there had always been young foreigners who came to this country to learn English, and she referred to me as an *au pair*. It was the only title I ever had, and I loved it. I imagined how much better it would have been to read: ROCKY'S SON MARRIES *AU PAIR*.

When the luncheon was over, Mrs. Roosevelt left with one of the students—in a Volkswagen! Only in America, I thought.

The next thing I knew the seminarians were holding a dance. Now my whole concept of sin and guilt, good and evil, became confused. I wanted to reject all I had learned, yet I didn't have the patience or capacity to understand all that Steven was learning from Buber, Kierkegaard, Tillich, and Niebuhr.

Religion became a sophisticated and a sore subject around our house. Steven placed the largest black Bible I've ever seen on our foyer table. (It was a magnificent mahogany table, given to us by the Klebergs, of the King Ranch in Texas, which meant nothing to me at the time. I just thought it peculiar for strangers so far away to give us such a beautiful present.) He always kept the Bible open, with a narrow satin ribbon, to the Twenty-third Psalm. Although back home I had never minded Mamma's religious pictures, I didn't like the Bible being displayed so conspicuously—it could be seen all the way from the elevator if the door was open. I admit that many visitors remarked, as soon as they entered the apartment, how nice it was to see an open Bible, but I went on complaining to Steven, loudly and often. Nevertheless, the Good Book remained open on the magnificent foyer table.

I began to worry that Steven might go all the way and become a minister. I thought I couldn't bear the extra burden of being the *Reverend* Rockefeller's wife, and hoped he would stick to philosophy, the lesser of two evils for me.

> *New York*
> *September 30, 1960*
>
> *Dear Mamma,*
>
> *Steven, Jr., was baptized at Union Church of Pocantico on Sunday. It is a cozy little church built by Steven's grandfather. Rodman and Tante Gudrun were the godparents. Steven proudly carried the baby to the pulpit.*
>
> *This week I met Crown Prince Harald. I thought he looked marvelous and spoke well. I am pleased to report that he was charming, diplomatic, and democratic. At least that is how my eyes saw him. He seemed a little bashful. Steven is the same with everyone he meets, and makes conversation so easily.*
>
> *Love,*
> *Anne-Marie*

The thought of meeting Crown Prince Harald was almost too much for me. Mrs. Roosevelt and the Norwegian Ambassador would also be there. Imagine meeting the "Man in the Castle" about whom I had been reading and dreaming since the age of seven.

I was so nervous when I arrived at the reception that I shook hands with the maid waiting to take my coat. She looked startled, and I was embarrassed. I didn't shake hands with Prince Harald—my hands were too sweaty from nerves by then—but curtsied Norwegian style. Mrs. Roosevelt was most gracious and seemed interested in the Norwegian Royal Family, all of whom had visited her at Hyde Park during World War Two. I wondered if all of us in the room hadn't wished to live in a castle at some point in our lives.

I was anxious to leave, feeling sure Steven must be disappointed by my lack of poise, grace, and ability to make conversation. But he told me, afterward, how proud he had been to see me look so natural and so very Norwegian.

Apparently inspired by having met Prince Harald, he got the bright idea that he should send for his Norwegian motorcycle. I talked him out of that by suggesting he would make a good cover story for the *Daily News* in his crash helmet. Later he did have it shipped over, though, and used it on the estate just once, to chase Mr. Moore's cows off the manicured golf course. But because of our baby he decided we needed something more reliable than his old convertible. Our first family car was a Volkswagen. He told me they were economical and easy to park, so he wouldn't have to pay expensive garage fees, and on snowy days he was pleased to point out that the Cadillacs and other fancy big cars were stuck all over town, while he easily zipped in and out of traffic.

New York
October 11, 1960

Dear Mamma and Pappa,
Please excuse me for not writing more, but I have been almost too busy to go to the bathroom. Steven is busy at his work and I am beginning to sympathize with widows.
We went to the United Nations to hear President Eisenhower speak. I saw Castro and Khrushchev. I don't know why Mr. Khrushchev was named "Man of the Year" in Norway, or why I

was named "Woman of the Year" with him. We do not have much in common at all. Fidel Castro looked as wild and ungroomed as any Norwegian working man. All that power in one room frightened me. Thank heavens I was with Steven.

Hearty greetings,
Anne-Marie

Later that fall Steven had to attend some conservation meetings at Caneel Bay, presided over by Laurance Rockefeller, and invited me to go along. When we arrived on St. John it occurred to me that I was now like the summer tourists back home, who came to Borøya for a change of scenery. The island "natives," like most of those in Norway, looked satisfied with what they had or didn't have. The guests here, myself included, spent a great deal of time on the beach, where the only strain involved was spreading various suntan lotions all over our bodies while we discussed how very hectic life was at home and how "exhausted" we all were. Still, I loved everything about my stay there, and when the time came to return home, I did so reluctantly.

Christmas seemed to come quickly that year. I took a trip to Kent to visit Betty, and we baked tin after tin of Christmas cookies. It was another pleasant respite from my mounting tensions, and my only problem was how to keep the oven temperature accurate. Back in New York, the holidays were filled with depression, and by January I knew something dreadful was happening to me. I began to keep a diary in which I could express all the terrible things that were haunting me and that could not be shared with anyone:

January 21, 1961

Please God help me!
Show me clearer that I have a good and loyal husband and baby to

be happy about. I see it, but I am too depressed to feel or show any gratitude.

January 22, 1961

We attended Riverside Church. I felt the sunshine through the stained glass window, but only for a few moments. Why not longer? Is it because of my basic selfish nature—do I expect too much—how much sunshine and warmth do I need, or give, for that matter? I am grateful for the few moments, but I seem to need more. I will try to look deep within myself for more answers if my emotions can stay intact, but that does not seem easy. My basic questions remain: Why was I ever born? What is the main purpose in my life? Is the world a better place because of me? If not, I hate You, God!! And I will not believe in You any more.

My emotions did not stay "intact." The spiraling depression worried Steven to the point of seeking professional help, and the family physician recommended a private hospital, the Silver Hill Foundation, in New Canaan, Connecticut. I didn't want to go, and the ride on the Merritt Parkway, in Steven's Volkswagen, seemed to take forever. As we turned off the parkway Steven stopped the car, slumped over the steering wheel, and sobbed like a child. So did I. He promised I would be home soon, feeling much better and stronger. He and Mrs. Conlon would take good care of Stevie. And he emphasized this was a hospital to which patients committed themselves voluntarily, where a fine staff of doctors helped many people to get through and over difficult periods in their lives.

I was surprised to discover in the morning that I was in another estatelike setting, with a main house and a cluster of smaller homes around it. Each "home" was for a different type of "ill" person. The main house, in which I stayed, was just like an inn, where patients with assorted problems, dressed in an understated and classic style that reminded me of Mrs. Rockefeller's, came and went as they pleased. Silver Hill had a place for physical therapy and an arts-and-crafts house, but I refused to participate in any of these activities. I understand now that this was part of my depression.

Mealtime conversations were sometimes on a high level. There were a few who didn't participate and seemed "out of it," partially from sedation or other drug therapy. They frightened me. I kept telling the doctor I wasn't sick, I wasn't like the rest of the people there; I was only feeling a little sad. He told me that many important people from enlightened backgrounds came to Silver Hill to be treated for depression, alcoholism, food addiction, and excessive cigarette smoking. (Even a prominent political figure had been there.) One very intelligent-looking man assured me that of course there was nothing wrong with *him*, either, but he had told the manager in a local department store that he was a patient at Silver Hill suffering from kleptomania. He received prompt and courteous attention. I often think of that story and feel tempted to use it during the Christmas rush at Bergdorf's.

After a few hours I felt that I'd had more than enough. After nine days I asked my doctor if I could go home. If I had to be confined in an estatelike setting, it might as well be Pocantico. At least there I didn't have a private nurse who sat watching me all day while she knitted dolls' clothes, who followed me to all my meals, and who hardly left me alone to go to the bathroom. I packed my clothes and announced to the doctor that I was leaving New Canaan by train that evening. He told me that ladies don't travel at night, and for the first time since I'd arrived there I spoke truthfully: "I don't want to be a lady any more." I was proud to have been able to be so frank and so openly angry, and the doctor seemed to understand.

The next morning Mrs. Rockefeller came to pick me up. Gently she urged me to stay, implying that if I loved Steven I would try to remain until I felt better. I told her I would have to prove my love to Steven in some way other than staying at

Silver Hill. Nothing she said made me change my mind. I left with the reluctant blessings of the director, who had tears in his eyes, and who gave me the name of a psychiatrist in New York City, Dr. Lawrence C. Kolb, head of the Department of Psychiatry at Columbia Presbyterian Hospital.

I had an appointment with Dr. Kolb the next day. After a brief interview he started to ask me questions about my parents, mainly my mother. I told him how close the ties were. I had some letters in my pocketbook from Mamma, which I translated for him, and he told me my mother herself sounded very troubled. I hated his words, and I wondered how he could base his opinion on a few letters. After that he started to ask me some very personal questions about my sexual life. I was horrified, and it was a relief when that hour came to an end. My next nine or ten sessions with him weren't much better. His insight frightened me. It was all most upsetting. I finally told him I didn't think I could see him any more. The trip uptown was too long, and perhaps he could recommend someone who practiced closer to my apartment building. The distance excuse didn't fool him for a moment, of course. He agreed that we all adjust and relate to each other in special ways—so, too, some psychiatrists are better suited to one person's needs than another's.

My next appointment was with a Doctor John Weber. I found it much easier to talk to him. He didn't make me feel defensive, nor did he make any diagnoses of Mamma. He never called me Mrs. Rockefeller, only Anne-Marie, which seemed significant and important to me. But he had a hard time getting me to say what was wrong, except for a vague though deep unhappiness and a feeling of insecurity. He tried another approach. Didn't I feel lucky as Mrs. Rockefeller? How many girls did I know who were as fortunate as I? Hadn't the Rockefellers accepted me into their family totally and without reservation? (It didn't occur to me until years later to think that Steven might be the lucky one.) His questions and my thoughts seemed to require too much effort on my part, and I didn't see how they could alter my craving for attention and signs of love from my husband that I could understand. I admit that many of my sessions with Dr. Weber were comforting and fruitful, and it really wasn't his fault that I went on feeling unsure of myself. And, at home, Steven became more intense in his study of philosophy as my mental powers of concentration dwindled. Soon I found that going to a hairdresser or to Elizabeth Arden's for body care made me feel better than seeing Dr. Weber. The hairdressers, who had eager ears and artistic hands, were very free with their compliments. They often said that they enjoyed hearing a rich and famous lady like me speak so openly, and they shared gossipy tidbits about some of their more famous clients.

Soon I was having my hair done at least twice a week, along with manicures and pedicures. I had to have my monthly allowance raised substantially, and Steven remarked that I was becoming more of a Rockefeller than any of the other women in the family. He didn't think my emerging glamorous image should be so important in my mind, and when he asked me to keep an itemized account of how I spent my money, I became defensive and annoyed. I didn't want him to know how much it cost for me to become beautiful. I wanted him to think it was all still natural.

On his twenty-fifth birthday, in April 1962, I decided to give him a surprise party. I invited every member of the older generation of Rockefellers to dinner in our home. I don't think this type of informal gathering had often happened in that family, and I don't think it has happened since. I cooked and baked for days, but managed to keep everything carefully hidden. And on the day of the party itself, I spent all morning being beautified from top to toe. I bought myself a long, silky, slinky green Japanese dress slit up the sides. My hair was dyed fashionably gray. I had a manicure, pedicure, and a facial. I couldn't wait to see Steven's reaction to the new me.

He was touched by the sight of his relatives and their various gifts to him, including a fat, flowery Mexican ceramic cat from Mr. and Mrs. David Rockefeller, for which Steven asked me to find a proper place in our home. But every time he looked at me, with a grin that conveyed his message very well, I knew he was in a state of shock. When the guests had gone home, he just turned to me and asked me to have my hair dyed back to its natural color, after I had returned my green Oriental "costume."

While New York State's problems were discussed by Nelson Rockefeller, and John D. III and the other uncles worried about overpopulation, and the whole family concerned itself with civil and human rights, I was busy wondering how to make myself more glamorous. I studied the slick magazines and drank in all the glamour of the women who patronized Kenneth's, Elizabeth Arden's, and Charles of the Ritz. I looked to the hairdressers for reassurance. I believed the Clairol ad that promised "only her hairdresser knows for sure."

• 6 •

Currents

Always having to guess how Steven felt about our relationship was frustrating to me. I can't count the times I asked, "Are you sure you love me?" or "Do you really care for me, Steven?"

"If marrying you, Anne-Marie, is not reassurance, I don't know what is."

I needed more than just words, yet my constant, unending hope for a truly loving response seemed to make it harder rather than easier for Steven to be demonstrative.

At times my pent-up feelings led to childish retaliation. Once I smashed eggs, a whole dozen of them, all over the floor in the study. Steven just ignored the mess, but the cracked old oak boards absorbed the eggs, and before long the room was filled with an unbelievably bad odor. It offended my nose if not his, and I was the one who called a cleaning service to come and eliminate that terrible stench.

Frequently I would call the seminary, have Steven paged, and joyfully remind him, "I love you. I miss you so much." After a while he asked me please to stop, because the calls, which he had to answer in front of the secretaries in the main office, made him uncomfortable.

"But I do love you, Steven."

"I know, and I'm grateful, Anne-Marie, but can't you please wait until I come home to tell me?"

One of the most embarrassing incidents started one day when we were sitting at the breakfast table and he was reading the New York *Times*. I happened to be wearing dark-colored lipstick, and I leaned over and deliberately kissed him on the forehead. He didn't notice my indelible kiss until after he got back from the seminary that night, and Stevie said, "Daddy, what is that spot on top of your head?"

"Never mind," I told him. "All those students of yours will just think you are a little more human. Maybe they'll even be envious, knowing someone must care an awful lot to wear lipstick for you so early in the morning."

But he was very angry, and it was four days before he recovered enough to forgive me.

I hated my feeling of insecurity whenever I tried obvious ways of winning Steven's attention, but I kept trying, somehow or other, to make my romantic illusions become reality.

"Wouldn't it be exciting for us to take some trips, Steven? Just the two of us?" I suggested. "Mamma could take care of Stevie, and we could go to a different country by ourselves." But Steven wasn't particularly enthusiastic about traveling at that point. We had plenty of time ahead of us to visit other countries, he said. He knew of too many wealthy people who tried to escape all their problems by taking one trip after another; but you don't come to terms with life by forever packing and unpacking suitcases. I persisted, though, in my idea that we should do more while we were young enough to enjoy each other, and finally Steven compromised to the extent of our planning one trip during the summer.

So in June 1963 I took Stevie to Norway, and proceeded to Italy, where Steven joined me. At first we enjoyed the beautiful city of Rome. I remember how we sat on the old Spanish Steps and watched the tourists go by. I remember our tour of the Vatican, where we saw Pope John XXIII being carried from the side door of his residence on an ornately decorated portable chair and platform, the *sedia gestatoria.* We followed the procession of people accompanying the Pontiff, and when I was stopped at the main entrance of St. Peter's by a guard who objected to my bare arms, Steven quickly gave me his sport coat. The Pope reached the main altar and turned to address the now quiet and respectful audience. His brief sermon, in which he spoke about peace and a compassion that transcended religious differences in the world, moved me deeply. I was surprised, too, because of the preconceived ideas about Catholicism I had absorbed from my Fundamentalist background. And although Steven never spoke in a derogatory way of any religion, he had said once that he wouldn't be willing to marry a Catholic girl. He told me about two of his Princeton friends, married to Catholic girls who had intended to leave their church but in the end had found it emotionally impossible to do so. Now both couples were caught in mixed marriages, which would undoubtedly multiply the problems that arise in any marriage.

Despite all the disturbing thoughts about Catholicism that passed through my mind, I felt strongly drawn to the Pope. Teasingly, I asked Steven if we should change our religion, but just as I posed that question he whispered in my ear, "Mia, look at that incredible face."

I turned to see a young woman in a nun's habit, with the most serene expression on her face: it seemed transfixed in an aura of holiness and purity.

I came across a similar expression a few days later, when we bought some post cards with reproductions of famous paintings of the Virgin Mary on them. Steven observed that Mary's face resembled his mother's at the time of her wedding. (After we were home, I asked to look at some of the family albums, and when I saw Mrs. Rockefeller's wedding picture I had to admit her face did bear some resemblance to the one on the post cards.) Every time I saw a nun after that, or looked at pictures of the Virgin Mary, I regretted that Steven couldn't or didn't perceive a similar expression of inner calmness and peace on my face. Whatever quality he admired I tried to incorporate into my being, usually in vain.

After a few days in Rome I tired of all the sight-seeing, all the overpowering religious atmosphere, all the places of "historic beauty and significance." My growing boredom stemmed from a lack of knowledge, as I was quick to realize and admit. Steven had been a history major at Princeton, and had taken art courses there as well, and he had been exposed all his life to good and serious artists, so it wasn't surprising that he loved Rome. The more he saw, the more energetic and enthusiastic he became.

"Everything I've ever learned has come alive here right in front of me," he said. "Everything means so much more!"

I thought he might be overemphasizing the art a little. There must be something more to Rome than what we had seen so far, I told him, and asked if we couldn't have a professional guide—even for just one day. Unfortunately, the guide agreed completely with Steven about the city's most impressive sights, and I didn't appreciate them any more than before—though he did compare my nose to that of Michelangelo's *David.* On our last day in the Eternal City my feet were tired, my eyes were sore, and I thought if I heard Steven wax enthusiastic about one more work of art I would scream.

Our next stop was Venice, where we went for a traditional

gondola ride. The gondolier sang romantic love songs and occasionally looked at me with a smile. Steven remarked that he would rather have the tour minus the singing and the attention we were attracting from passing boats, and he politely asked the gondolier to take us back to the hotel. When we arrived, the two men had a brief but spirited discussion. The gondolier's point was that since Steven had allowed his wife to dress attractively in Venice, he shouldn't object when anyone noticed.

Steven's only comment to me about Italian men was that they were interestingly candid but known for their unrestrained behavior toward women, especially those who were blond and blue-eyed.

"If that's true," I said, "when nobody wants me any more I guess I'll come to Italy, where I'll be sure to be appreciated."

We left Venice to go to Assisi. I was curious to see the places where Saint Francis had lived and preached and walked with his birds and animals. I was pleased to know something about this great saint. At a private dinner party in our honor, at the time we announced to Steven's parents our engagement, Mrs. Rockefeller had read aloud a very touching and beautiful prayer written by Saint Francis.

But the town of Assisi, which from a distance looked tranquil and picturesque, with its stone walls and tiled roofs, was quite different upon closer inspection. The courtyard next to the church was disappointingly dirty and in sad need of repair. There were birds, sure enough, but they were in dilapidated cages, not flying free, and weren't at all like my vision of the ones that had hovered around the saintly man walking on soft green grass. I left the courtyard and waited for Steven on the church steps, where I had a wonderful conversation with a guard. When Steven came out he advised me again that my actions were not always in my own best interest. He had a point. I'm easily disappointed by people for whom I should have more tolerance, and readily stimulated by people toward whom I should feel more reservation.

In order to compensate for my disappointment, Steven agreed to take me to a night club that evening. But Steven wasn't able to find any night club in Assisi, only a shabby café, with little tables outside but no live music. It wasn't his fault, of course. Still, that night I was annoyed at him, thinking he had the resources and imagination to find the best of everything that appealed to him in Italy, but not the interest to find one lovely and enjoyable place for both of us.

The next day we drove to Milan. There were hundreds of motorcycles on the road that morning, and the constant racket they made strictly limited our conversation. I thought back to our motorcycle rides in Norway and how it had been necessary to hold Steven tightly around his waist, and I somewhat envied the seemingly carefree young people whizzing by us.

When we arrived at our hotel, Steven began to make plans for sight-seeing. As soon as I heard the word I became exhausted and suggested that he proceed without me. I spent the whole afternoon drinking a large bottle of cheap Italian wine. It was the first and last time I ever did that. By the time Steven returned, I felt awful. He looked disappointed in me, and said, "Is this another feel-sorry-for-Anne-Marie day?"

It wasn't until Christmas that I realized his disappointment must have come partly from his having purchased a beautiful pink-and-white coral necklace for me that day, only to return to the hotel to find me moody and depressed and perhaps a little bit high. So he had kept the necklace until Christmas, even though we had a beautiful time making up. I was truly sorry, and expressed this physically and emotionally. That evening, we buoyantly walked all through Milan. At one of the intersections we came upon some kind of disturbance in the square, and Steven protectively grabbed me by the hand and led me away.

"Come on, Mia," he said, "we don't need that kind of excitement."

We found a cozy-looking place to have our dinner. While we were eating, a black cat that had been crouching in a flower box full of dusty plastic flowers overhead leaped onto the table between us. I jumped up in fear and screamed, but Steven didn't lose his aplomb and gave me a semilecture about getting so upset over trivial things. Even though we had enjoyed a good many of our meals and walks and drives through the countryside, this incident seemed a fitting conclusion to our stay in Italy. We decided to try Paris before we headed back to Norway.

But we had been in France only one day when I began suffering severe dysentery after having eaten some *escargots*. The attack came on while we were still in our car outside the large iron gates of Versailles. In the midst of my cramps, Steven told me that John D. Rockefeller, Jr., had given the funds to keep this historic palace as a French national monument. I never did get to go past the gates. I had to be driven back to the hotel in a hurry, and I spent the next week in bed. My illness did not dampen Steven's enthusiasm for the culture of Paris, though. He toured the city, thoroughly enjoyed his meals, and slept soundly at night.

"Steven," I asked him, "how can you sleep when I am hurting so much?"

"I must get my rest so I can take better care of you tomorrow."

When my mother met us at the airport in Kristiansand S, she said I looked like a cancer patient. For the first time since my teens I was down to a perfect size ten. So much for my expectations about travels to romantic places with Steven.

My urge to see everything and travel to interesting places didn't leave me, but the next trip I planned, to Caneel Bay Plantation in the fall, had to be without Steven, because he had gone back to his studies. I invited a close friend of mine, a Norwegian-American girl named Mette Strong, to accompany me. We had our own private house on the beach—the same one in which Lynda Bird Johnson later spent her honeymoon. It was a very tropical, lush setting, and we indulged ourselves in every bit of luxury we could come by. After a week of complete relaxation, though, I began to feel homesick and to miss my family. Somehow it seemed appropriate for me to knit Steven a white cableknit sweater to keep my hands busy during all the long talks with Mette Strong in the evenings.

We decided to leave a few days ahead of schedule. I arrived home unexpectedly, early in the morning, and went in to stand by Steven's bed. He was so startled by my presence that for one split second he didn't recognize me. When we went in to see little Stevie together, he didn't respond to me, either, until he heard me call his name. Then I received big smiles and hugs from both of them. It was good to be home, and we had a few weeks of uninterrupted harmony and peace.

Our period of tranquillity was shattered with the news that Governor and Mrs. Rockefeller were going to separate after thirty-one years of marriage. The headlines in the newspapers and the continual hourly reminders on the radio and television were most upsetting to me. I have always thought that separation and divorce were among the two worst things, emotionally and morally, that could happen to anyone.

Twenty-four hours after the separation was announced, sadness was compounded by tragedy. Michael was reported missing off the coast of New Guinea. That something bad could have happened to him was almost inconceivable. He was too young, happy, and sure of himself, and I was convinced everything would turn out to be a false alarm.

I can remember sitting in Tarrytown listening to speculations about how he might have been eaten by crocodiles or

· Nelson with Jennifer and Ingrid, 1967

Anne-Marie
in Little Norway,
Wisconsin, 1968
Bradshaw Mintener, Jr.

L. Roger Tu

Anne-Marie
campaigning,
1968

Anne-Marie with her mother outside Ormelia, 1969

King Olav at 812 Fifth Avenue, May 11, 1968, with Anne-Marie,
Happy, and Nelson Rockefeller
Wide World Photos

Anne-Marie and Steven at Pocantico Hills, 1968

Anne-Marie and the children with the Icelandic horse Gamlen

Ingrid and the Peruvian cook, Maria

© Dan Bu

Stevie and Jennifer by the fire

cannibals, or how he might have drowned, but I believed that he was probably off somewhere exploring on his own, completely unaware that anyone was concerned about his safety.

The Governor and Mary, Michael's twin sister, flew directly to New Guinea to investigate. Michael had been on an expedition with a friend, a professor from Harvard University, Dr. Rene Wassing, and the catamaran in which they were traveling overturned. Wassing, who was rescued while still clinging to the craft, reported that Michael, probably because he knew he was a strong swimmer, had tried to make it to the shore to seek help. After an exhaustive search into all the possibilities, the Governor sadly concluded that there was little tangible evidence that Michael might still be found alive, and he and Mary left for home.

Steven, Rodman Rockefeller, and I were driven in the official state limousine to the airport to meet them. The sadness engulfed us as the chauffeur closed the door, after Mr. Rockefeller and Mary entered the car. We began our journey to Tarrytown in silence, overwhelmed by a shared emotion that did not lend itself to words.

Then Governor Rockefeller squeezed my hand, and held it for a long time as he expressed deep gratitude to all of us for coming. He began to speak of his love and admiration for Michael and how it had taken courage for him to pursue his quest of "finding himself"—a quest that had led him to delve into the primitive society of New Guinea. Perhaps Michael needed to get that far away from his comfortable life in order to put his personal identity into perspective. Mr. Rockefeller seemed to be searching for a purpose in the expedition, and he tried to help us, as well as himself, comprehend the reality that Michael might never come back.

Mrs. Rockefeller's face looked grief-stricken as we entered her living room.

"Hello, Nels."

"Hello, Tod, how are you? I am sorry to bring such tragic news back to you."

After a long silence, Mr. Rockefeller carefully and slowly placed a large map of New Guinea on the floor in front of the fireplace. We all got down on our knees in a huddle to listen to his account of the futile search effort. The details were somber, painful, brief. We were able to grasp the gravity of the situation, yet we looked at each other with unvoiced hopes for a miracle.

As he was leaving, shaking his head in despair, Steven's father kissed Mrs. Rockefeller on the cheek and said good night to her and then to the rest of us before he left for the "Big House," where he had been residing since the separation. For some reason I thought of all the other times I had witnessed Steven's parents cordially saying good night to each other before Mr. Rockefeller walked to his private quarters. Now he had to get in his car and drive up the hill.

When his father left, Steven pulled his mother close to him and whispered kind words to her. He hugged and kissed her and said "Mother" in a tone of voice that still haunts me. I was happy for Mrs. Rockefeller at that moment because she had someone who could respond to her with a love that seemed tender, real, and nourishing.

My mind filled with thoughts about the possible meaning of the two catastrophes taking place within the Rockefeller family. Mamma wrote to me later that God was trying to tell the family something, and perhaps it would prove to be a way to reunite Steven's parents.

It didn't. Soon Mrs. Rockefeller was on her way to Reno to establish her six weeks' residence requirement for a Nevada divorce. I knew this was not something of her own choosing, and I admired the regal way in which she continued to carry herself—head always held high, with never a hint of desiring sympathy. Her bravery and stoicism in the face of the almost simultaneous loss of her son and her husband imparted strength to the rest of us. I knew that as a mother she must have had times when she allowed her emotions to surface, but they never overwhelmed her. When I asked her about her source of inner strength, she spoke of her unassailable belief in God. It was the first time she had ever confided in me about this aspect of her life.

On separate occasions, Mary and Steven went out to visit her in Reno. I wanted to accompany Steven, but Mrs. Rockefeller wrote to me that there was a world and a way of living out there that she did not want me to witness.

After the whole ordeal was over it was apparent that she had retained a sense of humor when she remarked, "Well, now I'll have more time for my children and grandchildren."

I think Stevie's question and his daddy's answer, a few years later, summed up my feelings about the divorce.

"Daddy, will you ever leave Mommy like Granddaddy left my granny?"

"That will never happen, Stevie."

Mary recovered enough from the traumatic events of the fall to go ahead with her plans to marry William Strawbridge, who came from a prominent Philadelphia family. The wedding was a joyous celebration for all of us. Billy seemed interesting and full of fun, and the prospect of sharing some good times with him and Mary was promising.

Soon after the Strawbridges were wed, Steven's father married Margaretta ("Happy") Murphy, also from the Philadelphia Main Line. The service in the little Union Church of Pocantico Hills was a simple affair. The Laurance Rockefellers held a reception for the new bride and groom at their home on the estate.

During the reception, at which no family members were present except for the host and hostess, Steven, Mary, Billy, little Stevie, and I went for a walk in the woods outside the main gate. It felt good to be in each other's company that day. Our marriages were just beginning, as was Nelson's with Happy, but for some reason their love reminded us how vulnerable we all were, and that didn't give us much cause for celebration.

Happy moved into Kykuit, the "Big House," with the Governor, and Mary and Billy took over the house next door to ours until they found a place in which to settle permanently. Mrs. Rockefeller began to look for a new residence off the estate. Her children encouraged her to stay where she had lived for thirty-one years, possibly putting in a private driveway or building a wall around her property. But it was probably too painful to be so close to the Governor and his new bride, who had been a friend of hers as well, because she soon bought a lovely country estate in Westchester County, which she named Sardana. No one could guess what the word meant or what its derivation was, and whenever anyone asked, Mrs. Rockefeller would smile and say, "It's a secret."

Whatever the secret was, the name seemed to fit.

Just as everyone was beginning to forget about divorce and remarriage, the whole event was revived in the news media when the Reverend Marshall Smith, pastor of the nondenominational Union Church in which Happy and the Governor had been married, was publicly chastised by his bishop. He had not checked the official church doctrine regarding the remarriage of divorced persons. Eventually, though, public interest faded. We resigned ourselves to Michael's death, and the dust from all the family upheavals began to settle.

It was after the turmoil had subsided that it became apparent that I was pregnant again. I wrote to Mamma and asked her to come to America to spend some time with us during the long languid days of summer before the baby was due.

"I must be going to have a little girl," I wrote to her. "This baby feels different and doesn't wake me up as often during the night with kicking as Stevie used to."

Mamma did come for a visit, and I felt sorry for Pappa and Torhild. By the morning of June 10, 1963, which happened to be my twenty-fifth birthday, I was feeling fat, uncomfortable, and hopeless-looking. The heat bothered me dreadfully. I began the day by writing in my diary, "I must be getting old and edgy before my time."

When I told Steven how I felt, he said no matter what age I happened to be I would always be beautiful to him, and added, "Don't you think that old trees are beautiful?" Then he started talking about the bonsai trees in Japan.

I guess I wasn't too thrilled at the prospect of being another year older, and when Steven and Mamma enthusiastically asked me to accompany them on an outing in the woods I emphatically declined. The two of them went off together, and after they returned they both became very busy in the kitchen.

When I walked into the dining room that evening, I thought their secret was the beautiful arrangement of water lilies Steven had floating in a crystal bowl as a centerpiece. I had never seen these beautiful flowers out of a pond before, and I was delighted and fascinated. For Steven to take something so intrinsically a part of nature and use it as a temporary decoration was both a meaningful and an extravagant gesture.

After dinner came the second surprise. Evidently Steven had picked enough wild blackberries for Mamma to make a traditional Norwegian birthday cake, or *bløtkake*, complete with whipped cream and decorated with berries on top. Mamma told me that Steven was responsible for the decorating and had done all the picking. After dinner, looking at his badly scratched arms, she told me that he must love me very much, and said, "I hope you appreciate his thoughtfulness."

The morning after the birthday celebration I came

downstairs to greet Mamma and Steven, who were already seated for breakfast. As I entered the dining room I stopped abruptly. Steven took one look at my face and then looked at the closed water lilies in the bowl.

"Let's put them on the porch, Mia. Maybe some sunshine will help to open them again."

He carried the bowl to the side porch, and I heard him explain the whole matter to Tusey, our golden retriever. "And don't go near the flowers, Tusey," he concluded. Steven always spoke to the animals in such a way that one would imagine they were college graduates.

I went out frequently to check on the progress of the flowers, but they remained closed. At last I realized that they had been better off in the tiny, muddy pond than they were with the candlelight, silver, and crystal, and I cried.

I threw the lilies in the dust bin, accepted the fact that I was another year older, and suggested a trip into New York City to Mamma. Steven was going to go to a military meeting, and perhaps Mamma and I could take a tour of the United Nations. On the way we stopped in Tarrytown to buy Mamma some comfortable walking shoes, but at first she refused to let the male shoe clerk measure her foot. In the end, grudgingly, Mamma allowed the man to fit her, and we were on our way with low-heeled shoes. We both needed them. Our private tour of the U.N. was long and interesting but very tiring. Before it was over I felt a wave of anxiety, thinking the baby might come ahead of time. I could only wonder what nationality it would be if it were born on the international soil, donated by Rockefellers, of the United Nations. As it turned out, my fears were unfounded, and we made it back to Tarrytown without any difficulty. But the house was lonely without Steven, even though Mamma was there.

I had to laugh when I thought about Steven and his military meetings. I never will forget, nor will Steven, the time he had to go to the Pentagon. As he was packing his suitcase he noticed that the trousers for his full dress uniform had not come back from the cleaners along with the jacket. He was unusually upset, so at seven o'clock in the evening I went across the street from our apartment to see if anyone was working late in the shop. Peeking through the large iron gates, I could tell everyone had already gone home. I tried to think of someone we might know with a pair of khaki pants and a thirty-inch waist, and decided it would be easier to get the owner to come back to the shop and find Steven's.

I decided to ask the police for help in finding the owner, and called our local precinct. The desk sergeant wasn't too solicitous about my husband's problem, but I was so persistent and called him back so many times that he eventually gave me the name Springer, though he refused to divulge the man's address.

After calling almost every Springer in Brooklyn, Queens, the Bronx, and Manhattan, I finally got someone on the other end of the line who didn't hang up when I asked if this was the Springer who owned a French dry-cleaning establishment.

We drove across town to the West Side. Steven rang the buzzer. We could hear that someone was up there, but obviously whoever it was didn't want to open the lock for us.

I tried to force Steven into saying who he was, but he just kept whispering into the intercom, "Mr. Springer, Mr. Springer." Finally I called out strongly, "My husband, Mr. *Rockefeller*, needs his pants."

The door opened for us, and we walked up five flights of stairs and saw a bewildered-looking blond woman, in a filmy negligee, who told us the man we were looking for wasn't in but we could leave a message.

On the way home I asked Steven why he always seemed reluctant to say his name.

"Because it shouldn't make any difference."

"Be reasonable—you must know that it does."

"Anyway, what did you think of that woman in her fancy nightgown and robe?"

"I sort of doubt that she is the original Mrs. Springer."

The next morning, before six, the pants were delivered by the doorman.

Steven finally returned from that particular Army meeting, and I was relieved the baby had not been born while he was away. Soon after his arrival we received a formal invitation to a reception at the Playhouse for the King of Thailand. When I saw that Benny Goodman was going to provide the entertainment, I asked Steven if we would be going. I was near the end of my pregnancy, and he didn't know what we should do and suggested we ask his mother for advice.

Mrs. Rockefeller thought it would not be in my best interest to attend the affair, from the standpoint of either comfort or propriety. She told me the Queen of England never allowed herself to be photographed while she was pregnant. At first I didn't see what that had to do with me, but then I took a look at myself in the mirror and saw her point.

"But please, Steven," I begged, "can't we go near enough to hear the music and see the King and all the guests?"

The night was enchanting as we walked hand in hand and barefooted over the soft green grass of the golf course. We saw the line of patiently waiting chauffeurs as we crossed the road on our way to the formal hedge at the back of the Playhouse. We tried to slouch down, which wasn't too easy for me, to make ourselves appear smaller. We found a hiding place that looked like a perfect spot in which to nest for the evening. We were thrilled as we snuggled next to each other until we sensed the presence of something or someone else. Looking directly at us were the cook and butler from the

Laurance Rockefeller household. It was a tossup which couple was more embarrassed as we all pretended that we had never seen each other. Steven and I settled beside another bush, where we were able to listen to and enjoy the music. When the tempo became oddly different, we knew the King must be leading the band. It was exciting and fun to play such games with my husband, and I wished we could share more times like this.

In a later conversation about the party, the Governor told us that the King had enjoyed leading the musicians so much that he, as host, had to figure out a diplomatic way of getting the baton back to Benny Goodman. In gratitude for such an enjoyable evening, the King presented Mr. Rockefeller with a huge, heavy, gilded, ornately carved elephant. Finding a suitable place for it in the Playhouse, where it was intended to repose, wasn't easy, because it didn't go with any of the furnishings very well. It ended up in the Card Room, on a round card table.

The two of us were thrilled when our daughter, whom we decided to name Ingrid, was born on August 13, 1963, at 2:42 P.M. Steven had called Mamma as soon as he arrived at the hospital to report on my progress.

"How long will it be, Steven?"

"About two år, Lovise," he tried to say in Norwegian. Even Mamma had to laugh heartily as she reminded him that in Norwegian år means "year."

Soon after I came home from the hospital, Steven surprised me by buying us a brand-new Ford station wagon. He said that with the two babies, a nurse, the diaper pail, and all the other equipment we were transporting now, we really needed a newer and more roomy car. I couldn't get over the obvious luxury of a car that was big enough for all of us—plus branches and flowers for arrangements and firewood, too.

Because we now spent so much time at our home on the estate, we both agreed it could use some decorating. Steven promised I could get rid of the dark Victorian wallpaper and some of the other features of the house that I disliked. I was excited about the changes I could make. After they were complete, I wandered down into the basement. All the junk that had been allowed to accumulate over the years and that I had wanted to get rid of was still piled up there. I made such a fuss about it that Steven, in a rage, carried everything up the cellar steps and out to the center of the road, where he threw it in a heap. We had to call for a groundskeeper to come quickly with a pickup truck to help make the road passable again.

After we were married, Steven had picked out a piece of land about five minutes from the gate, on a lovely hill. Years passed before he finally took title to it, even though it was family land and he had gone through family channels for the settlement. When the property did at last officially become his, he began to use his time on weekends to clear it by hand. He would often take Stevie, a natural builder, along with him. (Every time Stevie practiced "helping Daddy" with his blocks, it startled me that he began by building a pair of gates. When I asked him why, he said it was because he liked gatemen and hoped he could be one, too, when he grew up, because gatemen are always friendly.) The work took years, but the land was finally cleared, and with the help of an architect friend Steven had a one-room cabin built for himself in the middle of the property. It had a tiny kitchenette, a bath, and a large skylight through which he could see the heavens and the trees. Nothing there was very fancy except his ideas, which, as I imagined them, floated around the hilltop from branch to branch, like the birds.

During the time he was clearing his acres he would often suffer nasty blisters or painful rashes from poison ivy. I'm sorry to say that, instead of sympathy, all he received from me was indifference or even outright anger. I was too young then, and too recently married into a very wealthy family, to understand what drove him to such activities. He wasn't Paul Bunyan, I kept thinking, and he could easily have had the work done for him by some of the many employees of the estate. That, of course, was the very reason why he needed to do it himself. But I had grown up with people who needed to work hard just to stay alive, and I didn't want to feel like the wife of a woodcutter. I could think of so many more things to do on a weekend that would be a whole lot more exciting, anyway to me, than cutting down trees.

While the study in the woods was being built I spent my time thinking about the "dream house" we would share. Steven had agreed to hire an architect from Boston, his father's cousin, to draw up some plans for a beautiful house on a hill where "we could raise the children and grow old together."

Steven told me his cabin was coming in handy, and would prove to be useful as we developed our ideas about the house. He could study the effects of varying exposures to the sun and winds in different seasons. He could also get a better idea of how it would feel to be away from the confinement and protection of Pocantico's gates and walls and get along without the security of the estate proper, before we invested money and time and effort in building a house. Better to find out before rather than later whether we would like it. I conceded his point, but I also believed he needed a place where he could have more privacy and more peace and quiet for reading and writing, and feel free to surround himself with all the books and magazines and general clutter he liked.

His main concerns about our future home were how to keep the cost down and how to keep the children close to the master bedroom. I could understand his wish to keep the children close to us. He had always been separated from his parents' quarters as a child, and he was also somewhat concerned about their safety and felt that the closer they were to us the more protected they would be. Fears that would seem neurotic to most people—about kidnapping, for instance—are normal for the very rich.

I was mainly interested in my personal bathroom, about which I had many luxurious visions: lighted shelves for my collection of sea shells, cosmetics, oils, and perfumes; and a sunken bathtub where I could get away from everyone, just a little, when I needed to. Steven thought my bathroom embarrassingly extravagant, but he was slightly mollified when the designer told him the cost of a bathroom Jackie Gleason had recently had designed for himself exceeded the budget for our entire proposed home.

I continually made changes concerning the house in my mind, and Steven did the same on scratch paper. It was his form of relaxation, but he took it so seriously that I wondered if he would become an architect, too.

"Now I think I have designed the whole thing perfectly, Mia," he would say. "Just wait until I show you."

The sketches continued to go back and forth between Boston and Tarrytown until one year before we separated, when Steven decided to give up until he was certain about where his future would take him. At that point I began to wonder if the dream house would ever amount to more than the playhouse I'd had as a child.

We entertained more frequently now, and had taken over the place next door as a guesthouse, so Steven agreed to hire some extra help. Maria, who came from Peru, had a tendency to mispronounce names—she always called the Strawbridges the Strawberrybridges. Although she was not exactly the image of the perfect servant, we all came to love her, especially the children and Steven, for whom she seemed to have unlimited patience and feel a deep devotion.

Claire, whom we also engaged, was an attractive, intelligent, and highly competent American. Her main contributions to me in the years we were together were her sensitive companionship and her respect. On many of my down days she could get me to talk until I felt almost cheerful again.

With my added help I was able to keep the two houses looking like a picture book—tidy, cozy, yet not too formal. The food was prepared and served elegantly. The only things out of order at times were Steven's magazines and the New York *Times*, especially the Sunday edition, which he used to leave lying around unfolded longer than I cared to see. He often asked Maria and Claire to retrieve articles and papers thrown into the garbage before he was through with them.

By now I had studied all types of flower arranging, including the Japanese art of *ikebana*. The house was always filled with floral compositions of which I was quite proud, and I received many compliments on them, especially from Mrs. Rockefeller. I had thought Steven might appreciate the Oriental touch of *ikebana*, especially in the dining room, but one day he said, "Mia, you really ought to get a job running a museum. This is our home, which is meant to be enjoyed by all of us and look lived in, not arranged." I knew what he meant, but of course that did hurt a little. Besides, I really liked things my way—and I went right on doing things my way.

The only part of the house I carefully avoided was Steven's third-floor study, which definitely had a lived-in look, not to say a cluttered one. Every time I became brave enough to go up and take a peek, the sight made me shudder. I began to wonder if book publishers ever thought of making bindings that would come size and color co-ordinated, but to Steven it simply didn't matter whether or not his favorite possessions went together. In his little room were a bust of Robert Frost, an oil painting of the Grand Tetons, an etching of Abraham Lincoln, which looked very depressing to me, and the Picasso watercolor of the overweight nude woman putting on stockings, which he hung in his bathroom.

Steven may have resented some of our battles over tidiness and interior decoration, but he was always pleased by the many compliments bestowed on us. We saw different members of the family quite often now, especially Mary and Bill, who frequently came for supper. I thoroughly enjoyed their company. Soon, though, I became aware of growing tensions in the family because of the Governor's new marriage. It was at times awkward, for instance—or so it seemed to me—when Happy's children, who ranged in age from five to sixteen, referred to Mr. Rockefeller as "Nelson." No such informality toward any adult was ever permitted his own children. If any of them had attempted it, in fact, a family meeting probably would have been held to discuss what should be done about such rudeness.

The Governor's children, brothers, sister, and in-laws were devoted to Mary Clark Rockefeller, and their loyalty was felt and expressed in many ways. But in spite of all the confused and uncertain feelings, everyone was polite and gracious to the new Mrs. Rockefeller. Feeling slightly uncomfortable myself in referring to her as Mrs. Rockefeller, I just stuck to "Happy," and instructed the children to call her "Aunt Happy."

Happy came to our home for the first time shortly after Ingrid was born. She smiled broadly and said, "How terrific," when she looked at the new baby. Her tone of voice and her inflection were the same as Nelson's, and this caught me by surprise. She was smiling and friendly during the whole visit, and I assumed that must surely be how she came by her name.

I guess I wasn't the only member of the family who noticed the uncomfortable position in which many of the Rockefellers found themselves right after the wedding.

John D. III, for instance, began to invite the younger generation to private luncheons. He was an advocate of quiet strength through unity, like his father, and his deep care and genuine concern were felt by all of us. The subtle regrouping was a constructive effort on his part. It gave us an opportunity to express our opinions and experiences, which opened the way to a better understanding of each other and the family as a whole.

Among the young Rockefeller cousins, I came to admire John D. Rockefeller IV very much. I couldn't think of anyone else who could have carried the name better. I learned he had left college to go to Japan to study as an ordinary student. When he returned to the United States, he finished studying for his degree. Later he married an intelligent, beautiful, and charming girl, Sharon, whose father was Senator Percy of Illinois. They settled into a political life of their own, and switched to the Democratic party, largely due to the influence, I believe, of the Kennedy family. This break with tradition must have been as difficult for Jay as the decision to study philosophy and religion had been for Steven.

I can remember a personal discussion I had with Jay not long before his marriage. I gave him an honest opinion of marriage, based on my feelings about Steven and me. He listened carefully, but his knowing smile told me his love would conquer the difficulties that we had discussed so easily and freely.

Hope Spencer, daughter of John D. III, once told me how guilty she felt being pregnant and sitting at her father's table when he discussed the problem of overpopulation. Steven had great respect for his uncle, and appreciated the opportunity the family functions provided for sharing the knowledge each member contributed from his particular social interest. Every spring, members of the younger generation would bring their wives or husbands to a gathering called the cousins' meeting, to discuss serious matters, both personal and public. But I have to admit I found much of the conversation boring, and I never made a comment. Steven always pressed me to come along, but I never really felt a part of these gatherings. They were just not as relaxed or informal as Mr. Rockefeller's luncheons. I did invariably receive compliments on my appearance, but so did all the other ladies. It seemed to me that these young people had so much responsibility thrust upon them in any case that it would have been wise not to be so serious and tense all the time. I found it strange that Jay Rockefeller was the only person there who drove a fancy sports car, but great that he didn't feel guilty about doing so. Sometimes I wondered if the family had interests in the Volkswagen company, because the "Bug" was what so many of them drove.

The older generation of Rockefellers had its annual formal meeting, too, after the yearly Rockefeller Luncheon on Christmas Day. At the brothers' meeting, as it was called, the only woman in attendance was their sister, Mrs. Mauzé. Steven tried to explain what went on at these gatherings, and it sounded as impressive as the United Nations Security Council sessions.

The first Christmas after Mr. Rockefeller and Happy were married, we invited Steven's mother to spend Christmas Eve with us. Everything was prepared in Norwegian-American tradition. At the table Steven read the Christmas story from the Bible and prayed for both our families. After dinner I sang some carols as well as I could, accompanying myself with chords on the *harpeleik* Steven had bought me in Norway.

Christmas Day our family, along with Steven's brother, his sisters, and their respective families, assembled at 810 Fifth Avenue. Divorce and remarriage produce strange mixtures at holidays and family gatherings. It seemed ironic, for instance, that although Steven's father would not be there, he lived in the same apartment building, one floor below. I had visions of an elevator door opening and producing a blend of everyone.

Somehow, though, the concern and love that everyone felt for Mrs. Rockefeller, and shared that day, made me feel good. Adults and their problems were momentarily forgotten because of the joy of the grandchildren. And to this day Mrs. Rockefeller carries on the traditional celebration of the major holidays with all her children and grandchildren. It is a strong thread of continuity that they greatly value.

Briefly, tranquillity returned to our married life. But this was abruptly shattered one day, at least for me, when I saw a half-addressed envelope to an unknown doctor on our foyer table. When I asked Steven about the letter, he told me that he was now regularly visiting a psychoanalyst.

"Why didn't you tell me before?" I said. "Why haven't you discussed this with me, Steven?"

"Because I didn't know how to."

I became furiously angry—in fact, lost complete control of my emotions.

"Where is the strong beam in our household now?" I demanded.

Steven tried to make me understand that seeing an analyst was not a sign of weakness, and might even be a show of strength. He also said it might help us both in the long run. But I was far too upset to listen to any reasonable argument. I felt betrayed. I didn't believe him. I almost wished I had found out, instead, that he was having a love affair. I might have been able to cope with that disclosure more rationally.

I really became totally unreasonable with Steven over this matter, yet I could see he was not about to give way to me and abandon his plan for undergoing analysis. I told him I wanted to go away alone, without him. He didn't like the idea of my leaving him at this particular time, but my determination and headstrong desire left him no alternative but to consent.

I decided to go home. I was ready for another trip, and I thought it would be a good opportunity to take Ingrid along, so Torhild and Pappa could see her, too. Steven drove us to the airport. He was sad and quiet, but wished us a good trip as he kissed Ingrid and me good-bye.

While I was in Norway I couldn't get my mind off the fact that Steven was sharing his most intimate thoughts and our personal problems with a paid listener. Even though I could still hear him reassuring me that a good psychoanalyst does not alter the patient's personality, I was still worried.

"He just helps you to become more of what you are," Steven had told me, "and function better because you know yourself better."

I didn't believe that, either.

I wrote the doctor a childish and extremely rude letter, expressing my disapproval of the whole matter. After that, I gave up and tried to bury the man in my mind, as I would a bad dream. But I didn't want him to think I had problems more severe than a momentary tantrum, nor did I want him to discuss my "possessive-obsessive" personality with Steven, so later I wrote him a letter of apology.

It was during this stay in Norway that I was shocked, along with the rest of the world, to learn of President Kennedy's assassination. Steven wrote me a very informative and sad letter, in which he told me about his grief and about the regal manner in which Mrs. Kennedy had conducted herself, setting an example for the country. Steven also told me he believed President Johnson was a sound and capable man who would be able to pull the country together after this terrible shock. "As far as the Republican party goes," he said, "Mr. Nixon has the most to gain."

The letter also related how little Stevie had been mesmerized by the funeral services on television, and had asked, "Will they put you in a box like that someday, Daddy? Why would anyone want to kill the President of the United States?"

I was relieved that it was up to Steven to answer these childlike but difficult questions.

Before my stay in Norway was over I had begun to miss my home and family very much, and Steven's letters and the thoughts in them were comforting. Even though he was seeing a doctor, he seemed very much the same. It was also evident that he missed Ingrid and me. When I got off the plane to meet him, he told me that I looked rested and at peace with myself. He was glad I had taken the vacation and hoped my happy look would remain with me forever.

When I arrived at Tarrytown I felt welcome when I saw that he had decorated the living room with pine branches and candles.

For the most part the happy look did stay with me. Only occasional reminders of the doctor's presence in our lives, like the bills in the mail or the days marked in Steven's appointment book, caused me to feel pain and resentment.

One day, while I was having lunch with some friends, a package was delivered containing a baby bunting made of lamb's wool. When I saw how enchanted all my guests were with this standard Norwegian item, I thought of sending to Norway for one or two more for American acquaintances who were expecting babies. Then I had a brilliant idea: why not order ten and sell them? Within minutes, I decided to undertake a joint venture with my friend Naomi, who worked in her father's bookstore in Manhattan. At first it seemed like a joke, but then, after I telephoned Steven to ask about a lawyer, the matter became serious. Steven was enthusiastic, and the family lawyer I called told us we needed a name, a corporate seal, and a small amount of cash. With the information on paper, and the kind of excitement that goes hand in hand with the prospect of something new and exciting to do, we launched Namia, Inc.

We wrote to the manufacturer asking for exclusive permission to sell his product in the United States. We made him grand and naïve promises. Within a short time he granted us the right to be his sole outlet in this country. With the samples he sent, we approached the garment and purchasing offices of several department stores in Manhattan. The most enthusiastic reception we had was at Bergdorf Goodman. They asked for and received a year's exclusive in New York State on our product. We were so elated about closing the deal that we treated ourselves to a fancy lunch that probably cost the sum total of our net profit for the day. I also spent a large amount of our capital on photographs of Ingrid in the Kuddler, to use for promotion. I wasn't very professional about the advertising. No portfolio—only pictures carried in my wallet, which I brought out at the slightest hint of interest and displayed proudly.

Bergdorf's Christmas catalogue ran a feature on the Norsk Kuddler in a full-page ad. Soon a reporter from the New York *Times* called my friend and partner to ask her about our venture.

"How much money did the two of you need to become importers?"

Innocently and truthfully Naomi replied, "Less than a hundred dollars."

The next day the social page proclaimed that Mrs. Steven C. Rockefeller had gone into business with eighty-five dollars in the bank. With the article appeared a sketch of the bunting. Within months other manufacturers had copied the design, but they used synthetic fabrics and were able to sell the item at a much lower price. We figured that American mothers would not be interested in the quality or durability of the Norwegian wool when their babies could be kept just as warm in synthetics at half the price. Our business lost its momentum, and after one season we closed the books, eliminating some headaches in the process. The experience had been fun, and we wound up with no loss after expenses were deducted. I know now that I was not at all prepared for the real work involved in the project: the packing, the invoices, the meeting of delivery dates, and the storage problem. When we ran out of space in Mr. Cohen's bookstore, some boxes had to be kept in Pocantico. I thought about John D. Rockefeller, who had retired from making money at the age of fifty-four, and I couldn't understand why he had waited so long.

Not long after Namia came to an end, I told another friend who was visiting Tarrytown that I had a new money-making scheme. I did like having money of my own with which to buy personal things. "It doesn't seem right to use Steven's money to buy presents for him," I said.

"I couldn't agree with you more, Mia."

"Well, I am now hatching fertilized eggs and then selling the chicks. So far it's working very well."

That evening, at the dinner table, after the customary intellectual and philosophical conversations, I just sat back and smiled when my friend said, in all seriousness, "Steven, don't you mind those eggs in the bedroom with Mia?"

"I don't understand what you're getting at."

"Mia's new chicken-hatching, money-making venture. She thinks I can make a profit easily if I start to do the same thing in my house."

"Miaaaaaa."

"Steven, honestly, I don't know what she's talking about."

At that point they realized I'd been playing another of my simple-minded jokes. I told Steven if anyone was gullible enough to believe I was hatching chickens in our bedroom, she deserved to be a butt. Then I laughed like, as Mamma used to say, the sound of dried peas rolling out of a brown sack—endless.

After having carried the name of Mrs. Steven Rockefeller

for some time now, I decided it was inappropriate for me not to be a United States citizen. I asked Uncle Andres, because he had signed my guarantee papers on my initial journey to America, and my sister-in-law Mary Strawbridge to be my witnesses at the ceremony, which took place January 14, 1963.

When I arrived in downtown Manhattan for the event, I was surprised to find myself surrounded by foreigners. One man in particular always seemed to be going in the same direction as I. After a while I asked him why he found it necessary to follow me.

"Are you lost?"

"No, your face looks familiar, and I like it as well." His honest compliment put me at ease, and soon we struck up an animated conversation. He turned out to be a professor from the Rabbinical Assembly across the street from Union Theological Seminary.

My turn came for taking the oath of naturalization, and afterward a photographer bobbed up to take my picture standing next to a photograph of President Kennedy. Someone suggested that I hold the American flag. In my eagerness to do this properly, I picked up the pole with more strength than I needed, and the pointed tip got stuck in the acoustic-tiled ceiling. After the flag was dislodged, the pictures taken, and my papers picked up, my newfound rabbinical friend offered me a ride home in his taxi. I accepted, leaving Mary and Uncle Andres, who had their own rides.

As the cab pulled in front of the apartment building, the rabbinical professor observed, "Only in this great country could a meeting like ours take place."

We exchanged congratulatory good wishes about our newly acquired citizenship, and I rushed upstairs to tell Steven about my day.

He commented that I was like a sponge in the way I

observed new people and experiences, but he cautioned me to be careful about accepting rides from strangers.

"You were lucky this time, and met a gentleman, but please be careful in the future."

I was really proud of my Americanization, and thought I had the best of two worlds. I soon added to American statistics in another way—Ingrid was only a few months old when I thought I might be pregnant again. After my suspicions were confirmed by the doctor, Steven and I had a long talk about our apartment and the undesirability of raising three small children in the city and transporting everyone to and from Pocantico every single weekend. We decided to give up our apartment and move to Tarrytown full time.

One reason this decision relieved me was that I would not have to appear in Central Park looking pregnant, with one tiny baby in a carriage and another toddling alongside. Just the thought of those daily outings made me feel embarrassed. I am sure I'd had many pleasant days sitting on the benches in the park, but the lingering, discomforting thoughts are the most vivid.

The very first time I took Stevie to the park I didn't even know how to get the English pram off the curb, and while I was trying to maneuver it properly so we wouldn't both be struck down by the speeding Fifth Avenue traffic, I stepped in a large pile left by an early-morning stroller who had "curbed his dog." Barely holding back my tears, I had to ask the doorman to watch Stevie for a moment while I rushed upstairs to change my shoes, the whole time feeling guilty and nervous about leaving my baby downstairs. I finally got Stevie, who was dressed in beautiful and colorful Norwegian clothes, to the park. I sat down with some pleasant-looking women, most of whom turned out to be nurses, and the first comment, which still sticks in my mind, was "What family do you work for?"

Another time, I had just been given a beautiful mink jacket by Steven's parents, and I couldn't wait to wear that in the park. Stevie and I were dressed like ads from a Sunday supplement. No one could possibly have mistaken me for a maid or a nurse that day. Proudly I wheeled Stevie's carriage through the zoo. We went very close to the monkey cage, and a gorilla came up to the bars and proceeded to spit all over my face and my new coat.

I don't know why these incidents affected me so much, or why I couldn't have had a good laugh about life being the proverbial joke on all of us, but I just couldn't. I only knew I wouldn't miss Central Park much up in Pocantico.

Although I didn't miss Central Park or driving to Pocantico through the weekend traffic jams, I felt the absence of the excitement of the city and the friends I made in the eight years I had spent in Manhattan.

The children and Steven were thoroughly delighted with full-time country living. The study was readily available, and Steven was able to participate even more in the daily routine of the children, with whom he shared his love of nature. His patience and attention resulted in an increasing closeness to them, especially to Stevie, whose childish questions he pondered intently before answering. Sometimes these answers were simple. Once, when Stevie asked him about the love of God, he said, "If you understand how much your father loves you, then you may be able to understand a little bit about the love of God for all of us."

At other times his answers, although patient and thorough, were deep and difficult to follow, and I often wondered how the children could possibly know what he was talking about. There were times when he would discuss God and I would have to leave the room. I had my own doubts about Father, Son, and Holy Ghost, to say nothing of divine love and the hereafter, but I didn't want to spoil things for the children. I listened to Stevie's prayers only if

Steven was unable to do so. Even then I preferred to sing a little song of some kind, because I believe that songs express feelings better than spoken words.

Every Sunday, rain or snow, Steven took the children to church, sometimes carrying Ingrid in his arms. I accompanied them only occasionally. My vision of becoming a minister's wife was coming closer and closer to actuality. Many times I left the little church after Steven had delivered the sermon, feeling guilty that I could not share my husband's enthusiasm for the religious life. (I don't think I was the only member of his family who felt that way, either.) One day a caption in the *Daily News* asked my question for me: "Will Rocky's Son Go into the Ministry?"

Because of the tension between us on the subject, and his own doubts and uncertainties, he decided to get a Ph.D. in philosophy after graduating from Union Theological Seminary. He couldn't tell me how long that project would take. I was disappointed that his studies seemed to be never-ending, but I decided I'd rather be a student's wife than a minister's wife.

I made my first purchase of art when Steven received his Bachelor of Divinity degree from the seminary. I bought what I was told was a fine engraving by Dürer. Steven placed it in his study with his "special" things. I was proud to have chosen something that meant so much to him.

That Christmas, Stevie presented his father with an equally "priceless" charcoal drawing of some gravestones, with crosses everywhere—"Because my daddy works in the cemetery," he said.

In July, Steven, the two children, and I drove to Maine. On the way we stopped at Deerfield Academy to visit Dr. Frank L. Boyden, the long-time headmaster of the school. As he was giving us a tour of the campus, someone helped himself to my camera, which I had carelessly left on Dr. Boyden's porch. It was especially embarrassing because we had just been told about the strict discipline of the school. Dr. Boyden apologized and assured me that the camera would be retrieved and he would bring it to me personally in Maine.

But he arrived at Rest House, as the retreat in Maine was called, without the camera. He raised the subject only once, expressing deep regret. It wasn't as deep as mine, because I had just mastered the complex camera and become able to use it properly. While we spent some time together that afternoon, I was struck by similarities between the headmaster of Deerfield and John D. Rockefeller, Jr. I could see now why Steven admired him so much and why I was able to feel so comfortable and so much at ease with and at the same time so respectful of Dr. Boyden.

After our Maine vacation we went back to Tarrytown, where I anxiously awaited the birth of our baby. Steven began to study more, go to bed earlier, and (irritatingly) get up with Mr. Moore's chickens every morning. He told me I should try to get more sleep and follow the old adage that promises early to bed and early to rise makes a man healthy, wealthy, and wise.

Since I thought he had enough health, wealth, and wisdom to take a chance, I did everything I could to persuade or entice him to spend a few extra hours in bed with me in the morning. I told him the help would take care of the children and the house wouldn't fall apart without his beginning everything every single day. He reminded me that I wouldn't feel so sleepy if I didn't stay awake until all hours of the night with my music and thoughts and writings for my eyes only. He knew the only way to avoid my cajoling was to literally leap out of bed.

The children took after Steven, joining him in the early-morning chatter and noise. I tried to stay away from their cheerful din until after 10 A.M., when my mind and body were more able to tolerate such "uncivilized behavior," but I kept assuring myself that after the baby was born I would be able to turn over a new leaf and get up early like the rest of the family.

Jennifer was born on October 1, 1964. She was big—eight pounds, six ounces—and healthy.

"Congratulations Anne-Marie," read Steven's card on my night table in the hospital. I could see that our third child would look more like a Rockefeller than a Rasmussen. Her eyes were dark and her facial structure resembled that of her granny, Aunt Mary, and her father. Stevie was upset that he hadn't gotten a brother to play with, but his father soothed him by saying, "Nobody can choose in this case, only God."

Shortly after Jennifer was born I was sitting with Mrs. David Rockefeller, who looked at the Navajo necklace, the wedding present from Steven, that I was wearing, and exclaimed, "How extraordinary, Mia. Did you know that is a special piece of jewelry worn by Indian women and is a sign of fertility?"

That evening I took the necklace off, carefully put it in a box, and shut the box away in a drawer. There comes a point when even superstition helps.

The fall and the holidays that year passed without much fanfare. Steven and I made many of our Christmas decorations by hand, and had a beautiful Scotch pine tree strung with homemade ornaments. The next morning we were dumbfounded to find the downstairs a shambles. Our golden retriever, Tusen Takk, had clearly been busy during the night. He had chewed up some of the ornaments and distributed the remains throughout the first floor. This wasn't the first time Tusey had been so destructive. In fact, his bad habits were a joke at the family accounting office, which had received countless bills from me for fur slippers Tusey had eaten. However, this was the first time I took things in my stride and decided not to get angry about something already done. So we picked up as best we could and made the most of our day, starting our own traditions.

Steven presented me with a pair of solid gold earrings,

which I still wear almost daily. His tag read "Thank you, Anne-Marie, for the three, bright, beautiful faces you brought into this world."

Another tag said "This gift comes to you to remind you of my love, the hours we are apart." Inside that package was a beautiful and delicate watercolor of daisies. I cherish the painting and the tag, which is glued to the inside of my writing desk.

After the holidays, Steven and I began making plans to go to Norway with the children in the coming summer. My parents' home would not be large enough for all of us, and we began to think of buying a place of our own. It happened that a piece of real estate was available nearby. The house was tiny and run-down but had possibilities, and we decided to take a chance. Even if the house could not be rebuilt, the land itself was worth the asking price. We purchased the property jointly, and Ormelia, as the house was called—it meant "Valley of the Snake" because the constant sunshine in the area made it a perfect place for copperheads—was the only home we ever owned together. It had been the property of the district of Søgne and had been used years ago to house lower-income people. Mamma said that as a small child she had delivered milk there, and the people were too poor to pay, so the woman would put a spoonful of sugar through the window for Mamma. The irony of the young Rockefellers buying this particular property made good copy in the Norwegian press.

I went to Norway to make the house livable for my family. I had six weeks—and I couldn't resist the challenge. I called a builder who had a reputation as a capable craftsman and a reliable worker. He seemed dubious when I told him what I wanted done with the house, but he agreed to come and take a look before passing final judgment.

After assessing what needed to be done, he said, "Anne-Marie, this is in a pitiful state. Why don't you and your family move into my house for the summer, and we'll live somewhere else. Our house has a beautiful view of the ocean, and you can't even see it from this house. You were brought up on an island, and you should at least look at the ocean while you're home."

I couldn't be dissuaded. I asked him to send as many men as he could spare to begin the task of replacing the floors and building the bunks. The workmen didn't like the idea of making over such an old house, but they did the best job they could with it.

Little did any of us realize how much we would all come to appreciate that tiny and in some ways uncomfortable house. For instance, there was only one bathroom, with no tub, only a shower, and a cement floor and a toilet that did not function well. In addition, neither Steven nor I could stand upright in our bedroom. When he arrived, he took a few steps from the living room to the sleeping quarters and got his first bump on the head. But nothing dampened his enthusiasm. The close living quarters were probably good for us, and certainly they were different from what we were used to.

I would often stand in the window and watch Steven shift rocks around, in a continuing battle with our little stream, which overflowed every time it rained hard. He cleared the land behind the house, and chopped and stacked the wood neatly for the fireplace. He liked the way I passed him coffee through the kitchen window when he came down from the woods. Eventually we bought a piece of land adjacent to our property—to keep Steven chopping wood and to ensure privacy in the back.

Every corner of the house came to be filled with the evidence of happy times, from the shells, rocks, and sea-gull feathers we collected to the first picture taken of Steven and me, an hour after our motorcycle trip, which a reporter had given Governor Rockefeller when he came to Norway and which he had presented to us. This house was unquestionably the place where we spent the happiest and most fulfilling times of our marriage.

Steven took great satisfaction in collecting Scandinavian gifts to use as Christmas presents. I, who could never be as appreciative of embroidered pillows or hand-knit sweaters or decorated aprons or homemade cake as Steven was, thought many times that he would have made an excellent American ambassador to Norway. I still think so.

It had been a good summer for all of us, but when fall came I was happy to return to our home, which looked especially luxurious to me after Norway. It was nice to be back to a full staff of servants, which now included a secretary. I didn't mind living simply in Norway, but on the estate I wanted my life to be as comfortable as I could possibly have it.

Fall passed quickly as Steven worked in his study and I kept busy with my flower arrangements and my friends—and with renewed beauty appointments. The holidays were exciting this year because for the first time we were going to join Mary and Billy Strawbridge in giving a large New Year's Eve party in the Playhouse. Everyone's invitation stated specifically that he or she would have to perform during the evening. Mary and I had decided to be the Singing Nuns—I would play the zither and Mary would sing—but we had to abandon the idea because the clerk at the religious-apparel store refused to sell us habits when he found out we weren't real sisters. He thought we might use them illegally soliciting on the street.

Steven recited poetry at the party, but Billy Strawbridge's act was, characteristically, quite different. He disappeared for a while. Then Steven announced a surprise, and Billy jumped in through a window wearing only a white diaper held up with a huge safety pin, and a blond wig that belonged to me. (I had allowed him to borrow it if he promised to pay for the cleaning and restyling. It came from

Mr. Kenneth, who had matched it with my own hair, and I didn't dare tell either Billy or Steven it had cost $650.) At midnight a young Norwegian friend of mine, dressed in a white satin gown, entered the room. She had long blond hair and a crown of lighted candles forming a halo around her head. The lights dimmed and she sang "Santa Lucia" in a clear and beautiful voice. As one of the guests remarked, it was a blessing that the lights were low, because she believed there wasn't a dry eye in the room. For weeks after the party we received letters of thanks from our guests, telling us that the song had been one of the most beautiful New Year's Eve traditions they had ever witnessed.

The whole occasion was special for me because we had both worked with the Strawbridges, and it was our joint effort that had been most appreciated and that had given us the most pleasure.

• 7 •

Troubled waters

"Many beautiful feelings," I wrote in my diary on the morning of June 20, 1966, after picking Steven up at LaGuardia airport upon his return from a conservation meeting in Jackson Hole, Wyoming.

On September 28, 1966, I wrote only "Fairy-Tale Night," because no elaboration seemed necessary.

But by October of 1966 my mood was quite different. My feelings were like a Yo-Yo, and clearly at this point I was very down:

Will I ever feel free and contented again? The fleeting moments of peace have all but disappeared once more, along with my lust for life. I have many emotional sores that always seem to be aching. Where am I going with my constant dreaming? I have only one wish in front of me, and that is to be loved for what I might become. However, intelligence and feelings seem to be two different matters, each working in its own way, usually mutually exclusive. I must try to find a way out of my difficulties with my own resources and will power. I must become somebody in my own right, apart from anyone and anything in the Rockefeller family.

As if "being somebody in my own right" was my blueprint for happiness, I set out to follow every path that I thought would lead me to fulfillment as a complete person, a whole woman who would be truly loved and cherished by the seemingly unattainable Steven.

I started to take more and more lessons. First the guitar. I didn't believe I was particularly gifted in that area, but Steven kept assuring me that if we ever had a depression I could support all of us by singing and playing in coffeehouses. I had my doubts about being a musical entertainer, but, half-seriously wondering what I could do if we ever needed money, I decided I could be a taxicab driver. My driving had become so aggressive, and I was so sure of myself behind the wheel in Manhattan traffic, that I knew I could make a good day's wages as a cabby. Besides, I had always found cabdrivers friendly, inquisitive, and the only group in American society who freely spoke their minds. It seemed to me that their lives could never be lonely, and more than once I really did think about applying for a license.

My interest in Japanese flower arranging continued, and I enrolled in a course in *ikebana* at the Ikebana Art Center, where the lectures were in Japanese but translated into English. I took additional courses in flower arrangement and joined a new garden club whose members had a particular interest in the subject.

Someone told me about an arts-and-crafts course being offered at the Riverside Church, and I enrolled in that, too. This introduced me to the joys of hand weaving, and I became so interested that I took private weekly lessons from the instructor. Soon I was proficient enough to want my own loom, and in my dwindling spare time I wove several scarves and neckties, and some silk material, from which I made an evening bag.

I always seemed to stumble onto something new and useful to learn. One day, when I was shopping, a particularly beautiful and highly unusual pair of cuff links caught my eye. I was so taken by their quality that I purchased them and immediately inquired about the artist who had made them. With only his name and my detective's instincts, I was able to track down a retiring old Russian gentleman, Dr. Winogradow. He was astonished when I called on him—at first by my interest, and then by my persistence in seeking him out.

For an eighty-year-old man, Dr. Winogradow was surprisingly young in looks, spirit, and mind. He stood very erect, and his handsome profile ended in the neat triangle of a trimmed beard. His hands looked delicate, yet they were strong and steady when he shook mine. His voice was calm and deep as he enthusiastically told me the tale of his "new art form."

He had been a chemist for a long time but had always felt an inclination toward the visual arts. One day in 1935, while he was holding a transparent sheet of acrylic against the light, he noticed a flaw in the material. He said this bubble "appeared luminous, like a shining star against the uniform dark-colored background." I felt that everything he told me should have quotation marks around it and be recorded for posterity. This bubble, he explained, "this tiny intruder, signaled an idea." For two years he studied the bubbles and developed techniques for producing them deliberately. In time, he told me, he had become able to lay out designs and shapes in the plastic with gold filigree, and fill the indices with color. Eventually he produced a gemlike mosaic, which was exactly how I would describe the cuff links I had bought.

I begged him to tell me more, and asked him why I hadn't heard of his work before.

This chemist turned artist, now fast becoming my friend, went on to say that he called his art form inlonné because the word suggests an affinity to the ancient French and Oriental art of cloisonné. Dr. Winogradow said he had spent all his time since 1937 developing and refining his technique. Impressed by his tenacity and patience, I asked him if he could teach it to me. "Please," I said, "I must know how you do this."

How much I would gain, I thought, if this wise man could impart some of his knowledge to me.

He told me that so far only he had fully mastered the craft, but he had been thinking of teaching it to a younger person, artistically inclined or with an aesthetic sense, who would carry on with it after he was gone.

Dr. Winogradow took a chance with me, and I did become his student and disciple. I enjoyed every visit to his apartment, which he shared with his gracious, interesting, and kind wife. To have become really expert would have taken too long, but after two years of study I had made enough progress at least to appreciate the genius that he possessed and comprehend the time and effort that must have gone into his larger works of art.

I asked him if he had ever had a one-man show. He told me that except for a Museum of Natural History display of his inlonné pictures based on Mayan themes and his compact and jewelry sales at Georg Jensen and the America House, his art was not generally known to the public.

Steven also appreciated the charm and the special quality of Dr. Winogradow's work, and when I told him I thought more people should be exposed to inlonné, he agreed that we could sponsor a show for my teacher. After some searching, we found a gallery that was more than delighted to exhibit all seventy-five pieces that were then available.

At first Dr. Winogradow was reticent, shy of the publicity that goes hand in hand with such an undertaking. He was also reluctant to part with some of his favorite pieces, and put a high price on them.

Various members of the Rockefeller family, personal friends, and the public in general turned out to see, admire, and buy inlonné. Dr. Winogradow's work received well-deserved public acclaim, but some of the headlines played up other aspects of the show:

CINDERELLA EMERGES AS ART PATRON

SHY WIFE COMES TO NEW YORK ART SHOW

And, from Chattanooga, Tennessee:

SOVIET ART IS PUSHED

I continued my studies with Dr. Winogradow until he died in November 1970.

There was no question in my mind, or Steven's, either, that I did have some artistic abilities, but even with all these lessons I was taking and the accomplishments resulting from them, I was still lacking something.

One day a friend told me that a Scandinavian was teaching a course called "The Science of Creative Intelligence." I became interested immediately. Perhaps someone from my own background could understand how my mind worked or why it didn't work, and with this understanding he might be able to teach me how to be creatively *intelligent*.

When I met the gentleman, he assured me that it would not be difficult to give me the tools whereby I could develop, in a natural way, my full mental potential. He promised that the transcendental meditation I was going to learn would have spontaneous and automatic results. I looked forward to the "deep relaxation, more energy, greater efficiency, better health, rejuvenation, harmony, and peace of mind" that would soon be mine. He reassured me that the technique was not some kind of trickery or sham, but that in fact transcendental meditation was fully supported by modern science and was being taught in some universities and colleges, and even in some high schools.

When I suggested that I might not be equipped to acquire such a complicated scientific skill, he told me that anyone was capable of learning the technique, regardless of race, creed, or color. How strange that this was still a semisecret, I thought. Imagine everyone being equally gifted!

I was most excited by the prospect of instantaneous results. Think of poor Steven, who had spent all those years with hundreds of books in his musty study trying to achieve comparable goals.

On my first day of learning transcendental meditation, when I was promised initiation and graduation all at once, I was like a girl entering her first day of grade school—breathlessly excited and hopeful, intensely curious, and anxious to get on with the learning. The teacher said that the program was a matter of experience and not intellectual appreciation, and it was only moments before that he had assured me he observed the first effects on me. He convinced me that I could feel the results myself, and I must admit to a calmness and evenness of breathing that I hadn't known for a long time, if ever. Unfortunately, in the place where results mattered most to me—at the table that night during dinner—they were not noticeable.

In time, the new breathing techniques did help me relax and sleep better, and my swimming improved immeasurably, but that was the sum and substance of my venture into the Science of Creative Intelligence.

Perhaps I still hadn't hit upon the right field of study. I scouted around and asked questions. Someone told me that what I needed was a course called "The Art of Conversation," and I was in luck, because such a course was shortly to be given at the Regency Room in Delmonico's Hotel.

Why not? If I could master dinner-table conversation and become able to respond to Steven on his own high plane, that might give me the key to success in our marriage. So at the appointed hour I made my way to the Delmonico Hotel.

The first person who spoke to me at the meeting was a woman who didn't seem to need any help at all in conversation. She talked a lot, about everything under the sun. And everything she wore, from her white gloves to her garden-party hat, conveyed the message that she was a social, correct "lady." At home that night, I told Steven I had met a type of woman that day who was definitely not to my liking.

But at our second meeting I was in for a surprise. My extremely proper new friend, still with her dainty gloves on, began to talk about the Tarrytowns. It turned out that she, too, lived there, and had begun to be concerned about the community's sad environmental decline. Imagine someone looking the way she did and caring if there was litter in the streets. I decided she was Westchester's answer to Lady Bird Johnson, and when I began to show interest in the subject, she asked if I would care to join her civic project.

After I arrived home I called an acquaintance and asked about "Mrs. Conversation A-plus."

"Of course I know her, Anne-Marie. *Everyone* knows and loves Mary Jane." Soon I finished the amusing course in the Art of Conversation and went back home, where I was to learn more about litter and pollution. It seems that both Tarrytown and North Tarrytown were afflicted.

After I had studied up on the alarming state of affairs in the Rockefellers' own back yard, I went to a meeting to which the four antilitter committees of garden clubs of the two Tarrytowns were invited. Before the meeting, I suspected that I had been included because my name was Rockefeller. Afterward I decided it was because of my age, the group being in need of youthful energy to carry out its lofty ideals. Much later I discovered it was because I was genuinely liked.

When the outline and the goals of forming a new and unified committee were presented, I was fascinated. I found out that Tarrytown was the heart of Washington Irving country and the site of many other historical landmarks. We all agreed that people coming to visit these restorations should be able to take away a pleasant memory of a clean community, a place where residents have pride in their heritage. No group of Scandinavians could have been more excited about making things clean and setting an increasingly shabby community to rights again.

I talked the whole thing over with Steven, and we both decided it was a worthwhile venture into which I could pour my organizational energies and my "beautifying" talents. An artist friend co-operated by designing a poster depicting a Dutch girl called Katrina, who implored HELP KATRINA KEEP OUR TOWN CLEAN.

When the design was finished, Mary Jane and I took it to the family offices in Rockefeller Center for suggestions about a printer. We were directed to someone capable, and with donations from fellow members we were able to pay for six hundred color reproductions of Katrina, which were then disseminated around the Tarrytown area.

I began to enjoy the companionship of my new Tarrytown acquaintances. Not only did they like my ideas and appreciate my energy; they enthusiastically did everything they could to encourage other young people to join the crusade.

One day Mary Jane and I decided to take one of the posters to the New York headquarters of Keep America Beautiful, Mrs. Lyndon Johnson's project. They were so pleased that they promptly hung it up for display. They also requested flyers with our motto, which was a good idea, even if we had to rush out and have five hundred printed on the spot. I took the liberty of sending some to various members of the Rockefeller family, urging them, too, to support our cleanup campaign. I included a reminder that industrial leaders of the area might pay more attention to their responsibility if they knew that the Rockefeller family was interested in the beautification of the countryside and village in which they spent some of their time.

I also wrote to Governor Rockefeller concerning the accumulated debris along Route 9, especially the portion adjoining the Sleepy Hollow Cemetery, which was itself in a deplorable condition. Fortunately the state highway department cleaned up the roadside litter just before Memorial Day weekend that year.

I did what I could for the cemetery, too. The actual site of Washington Irving's grave was pitiful. If only some flowers and grass could be coaxed to grow there, I thought—and then I had a bright idea. What better place to find rich topsoil than the Pocantico Estate itself? I asked the head gardener for enough for one grave site, and although he was confused by such a strange request, he contributed what I'd asked for. So it became possible to provide poor old Washington Irving with a proper setting.

In the late fall, in order to get our mailing campaign off to an auspicious start, we staged a wonderful parade through the village, complete with Dutch girls, Boy Scouts, Girl Scouts, the fire department, and the mayors of the two adjoining towns. The Salvation Army served us doughnuts and coffee.

A few days after the parade, Mary Jane and I bought some lovely chrysanthemums from a local nursery and planted them along the main street in Tarrytown. Our committee was becoming a familiar sight in the business district as the members walked along the sidewalk picking up litter and urging merchants and passers-by to do so, too. I was not unaware of the influence my last name had on proprietors, and if I found a particularly messy area I would simply enter the nearest shop, stick out my hand, and say, "Hello, I'm

Anne-Marie Rockefeller. Won't you help us with this litter problem?"

Never before had my efforts been put to such good use. Our funds were ebbing away when I got another idea. I could use my Namia contacts at Bergdorf Goodman to persuade the store to have a fashion show for us. Bergdorf's willingly agreed to put on a show of children's clothing in conjunction with a luncheon we would arrange. Mrs. Laurance Rockefeller, who accepted an invitation to be our guest speaker, took as her theme the goal of our committee, which was to preserve the beauty of Sleepy Hollow country.

Mrs. Lyndon Johnson sent me a telegram, which was read at the fashion show:

HOW SPLENDID IT IS TO LEARN THAT YOU HAVE FORMED A COMMITTEE TO ASSIST THE BEAUTIFICATION OF THE TARRY-TOWNS. SO MANY THINGS CAN BE ACCOMPLISHED BY THOSE WHO ARE ALERT TO THE POTENTIAL OF THEIR COMMUNITIES. BEDS OF FLOWERS, WINDOW BOXES, SHADE TREES, NEW TRASH RECEPTACLES, ATTRACTIVELY SCREENED PARKING LOTS, AP-PEALING PEDESTRIAN AREAS.

THE POSSIBILITIES ARE ALMOST WITHOUT END, AND ALL LEAD TO A NEW AND VISIBLE WORTH IN ONE'S HOME TOWN.

WITH BEST WISHES TO ALL IN ALL THAT YOU DO.

SINCERELY,

MRS. LYNDON B. JOHNSON

Our fashion show was a success, and the proceeds and publicity were a boon to our cause. With some of the money, we purchased park benches made by the inmates at Sing Sing. We also discovered that New York City's litter baskets were made in Astoria, Queens, and went directly to the source in order to save money on the twenty we needed. The Board of Trustees of the Tarrytowns authorized the use of the municipal garbage truck to go to Queens to pick them up. Mary Jane, impeccably groomed as always, went along in the truck, and as the unlikely-looking duo drove off, I called out, "You forgot your white gloves!"

Because of my involvement with the Beautification Committee, Governor Rockefeller invited Steven and me to accompany him on a Circle Line tour up the Hudson with Mrs. Johnson and Mr. and Mrs. John Lindsay. For much of the time I was engaged in an engrossing conversation with a nice gentleman sitting next to me. The two of us spoke about the historically interesting homes in the area around Tarrytown. I told him one of my favorite places was the Gothic-looking museum, Lyndhurst, the former residence of the Gould family, which nowadays didn't seem to be properly cared for. Many things needed repair, I told him; the greenhouses were in especially bad state, and I had ideas about a good many other matters that should be taken care of.

The Hudson tour finally stopped at Irvington. A chauffeur met us, and I accompanied Mrs. Johnson, who was to be the guest of the Laurance Rockefellers for the evening. She was very gracious and easy to talk to—among other things, she thanked me for the work I was doing on the Beautification Committee, and I felt honored by her kind words.

One week later I received a letter from the gentleman with whom I'd talked on the boat. His name was James Biddle, and he invited me to join the Lyndhurst Council in the hope that I could put my ideas for the museum into practice. I was delighted to accept, and spent the better part of two years on the council.

I wasn't the only Rockefeller joining committees and espousing causes. The Strawbridges supported the Urban League, and because of their involvement, Steven and I were invited to a dinner dance for the benefit of the Westchester Urban League, which was held at the Playhouse.

We sat at a small table with Ann and Bob Pierson, Mary and Billy Strawbridge, and an attractive young black couple from White Plains, Mr. and Mrs. Lionel Stevens. We had dinner served around the pool, which reflected the soft lights and the terrazzo floors. It was a relaxed and informal group; after dinner I gravitated to Steven and perched myself on his lap, and there was a lot of good-natured "couple talk." A pleasant evening altogether—how sad that all four couples are now separated or divorced.

Not long after the dinner dance, our new friends invited us to an evening party at their home in White Plains. I wrote that Steven and I would be delighted to attend, but wondered if they really meant it would begin at 10 P.M.

Never having been to such a late party before, we made a point of arriving at ten o'clock sharp. It took so long for someone to answer the door that we thought we had come on the wrong day. Not another car was in sight. Afterward, our hostess confessed that when she heard the doorbell ring she was surprised that any of her friends would come so early. Then she remembered my puzzled question, and said to her husband, "It must be the Rockefellers."

The party was fun and the most relaxed occasion Steven and I had been to in a long time. After that, I invited my new friend to the Playhouse, often with her children, and we had a most enjoyable relationship. Through her I made many other black friends. One man, who had formerly been an FBI agent, said that the first time he was invited to the estate he had told his sister where he was going and asked her to call the police if he didn't return by morning. What had worried him was that the Rockefeller enclave was not only independent of the local police force but also entirely beyond the province of J. Edgar Hoover!

One day, at a gathering in a friend's house, Steven and I were introduced to James Meredith. Mr. Meredith and I had some difficulty understanding each other, especially when he informed me that if I was seriously and truly for integration I would not associate with certain friends of mine who did not share my liberal views. I did not concede his point, or maybe I didn't want to, because this would be like saying good-bye to half my world, if not more. Also, I firmly believe that one can be constructively influential with certain friends.

I had always admired Mr. Meredith, who publicly displayed such courage and determination as he solitarily took his own personal stand against prejudice. I envied his strength, perhaps because I wished I could be as strong myself.

When that gathering ended, one of the guests had some trouble starting his car. Steven went to help, and the sight of him, along with three large black men, pushing the disabled Volkswagen, would have made a good and interesting picture—if only I had had my camera along!

On the way home, Steven objected to my having had such a long and engrossed conversation with James Meredith. The little disagreement seemed to be forgotten quickly, as most husband and wife squabbles are, but left me feeling that some personal and important aspect of myself had been infringed on again.

Steven had in fact long been a supporter of the Civil Rights Movement, and he was also interested in cultivating our new acquaintances. He loved having guests come to our home for dinner, and trying to understand the experience of being black. Our growing involvement with civil rights issues permeated the whole family. Later, even little Stevie wrote a composition on slavery:

The first Dutch ship that brought the slaves to America was the *Jesus* ship. It was strange because Jesus was a good man and the *Jesus* was a bad ship. . . . The slaves were used because the Englishmen were not used to doing work. . . .

Abraham Lincoln signed a piece of paper that was called the Emancipation Proclamation. It meant the slaves were free. But they were not really free because they could not go to school with white people. . . . Now slavery does not exist because of some black people who wanted freedom, like Dr. Martin Luther King.

Steven talked a lot about the black dilemma, the black experience, existential dilemmas, and revolution. The social significance of civil rights was monumental, he said. I didn't really respond to any of the intellectual posturing, but could intuitively understand something about the personal hurts that my black friends had endured. I found a need in them not unlike mine, and that was the search to know themselves fully, so that the society in which they lived could know them and accept them on their own merits.

Also, the tension and excitement I sensed in various discussions of conditions in the country and what was to be done about them reminded me of the atmosphere I had felt as a young girl during the war. Some of the stories I'd overheard then, about atrocities perpetrated on Jews and other minority groups, and the long nightmare of injustice and terror, were not very different from the stories I heard about segregation and prejudices here in this country. I know what it is to be instilled with fear. All the islanders felt it, even the children. One day, when the Gestapo ordered Pappa to take out one of his boats to pick something up, I went along, promising to stay below. I couldn't resist peeking though, and for a long time all I saw was a wet green coat. Then I saw a large brown boot kick the limp, wet green mass on the floor, and I knew Pappa had gone out to pick up a body. I remember all the strangers who took refuge with us on Borøya and how Pappa finally had to throw some ammunition he'd been hiding into the sea because the danger seemed to be closing in on us. I also remember my ambivalent feelings toward the Germans. I liked hearing the marching and the clicking of the beautifully polished boots as they hit the street, and was secretly filled with excitement when I heard the loud and joyous cadence calls and the singing.

All of these feelings and thoughts seemed to slip back into my consciousness as I listened to Whitney Young, Martin Luther King, or a dynamic young worker, Candy Latson, at the Phoenix House. A battle was being waged, and, as usual, I could see both sides of the issue. My emotional involvement and the resulting excitement provided a kind of locomotion away from my own personal conflicts. I was moving, but toward what I did not know.

Just as I had in my childhood, when the lighthouse keeper promised to fly the Norwegian flag as soon as we were free of the Germans, I kept looking all around for a sign of victory—only this time victory meant becoming somebody. But the more assiduously I tried to commit myself to causes, committees, and courses, the wider the gap became between Steven and me as husband and wife.

In June 1967, Steven was asked to deliver a commencement-day address at Marymount College, in Tarrytown. His speech was clearly an example of the different way he and I approached issues and ways of dealing with them. But I could also see that his talk that day was filled with indications of his own inner struggles. He stated that the world is filled with a restless energy, a search for "social, political, and economic environment. For many individuals it is also a search for and the discovery of happiness, purpose, and changing social mores." Even the language describing religious values is changing, he said. "For example, what Christians have in many cases traditionally called forgiveness is today, under the impact of psychiatry, better understood by many people as acceptance."

Surely that is how I perceived the influence of psychoanalysis on Steven. Forgiveness at least is filled with emotion. It implies anger and then love. Acceptance, the way Steven meant it, was devoid of feeling—and feeling was something I needed and still wanted so desperately. But if Steven's doctor had influenced him, so had the Civil Rights Movement, and he spoke of that, too, during his address.

The Civil Rights Movement was born and captured the imagination and excitement of many of the nation's finest young people, who saw only too clearly the inconsistency between their fathers' eighteenth-century ideals and the social injustice which they had allowed to grow up around them. . . . The Civil Rights Movement seemed to have awakened America's moral sensibilities, and effectively channeled some of her youthful energy. Its most vocal and responsible leaders remind one of the prophets of ancient Israel. Once again history seemed to be thrusting upon America an obvious domestic problem, and many stopped worrying about our national purpose and started writing, marching, and organizing for the cause of equal justice.

Then, in 1960, President Kennedy was elected, and he began to articulate forcefully many of the aspirations and the ideas that had been taking shape in the minds of his countrymen. Kennedy called on America to move again into a new adventure, and many liked his vision, and America began to move into the future with a new sense of mission and excitement. . . .

The Johnson victory over Goldwater seemed to confirm the direction that America was now heading, and the Poverty Program became a new sign of the direction. Then a dark cloud appeared on the horizon: Vietnam. And the cloud became a storm and the storm became a hurricane, and the whole world waited tensely in the fear that this terrible creation would veer in their direction and engulf them all. . . .

I can remember giving an outraged speech in college over our failure to intervene in the Hungarian Revolution of 1956. . . . Perhaps Eisenhower's caution for the sake of world peace was justified. I do not know. Again, today, I certainly would support whatever we have to do in order to defend the rights and independence of Israel. However, if I was sent to Vietnam I would be haunted by questions as to the justice and intelligence of U.S. policy. . . .

Loyalty to one's own nation is a virtue, but blind patriotism and extreme nationalism are among the evils that currently plague mankind. . . .

Although there are some very belligerent Communist nations, our major enemy is no longer international Communism. It is clearly poverty, ignorance, social injustice, overpopulation, race hatred, and international lawlessness. . . .

The restless energy we often feel in ourselves and we see all around us today is not in itself necessarily good, and is in fact often purely destructive.

I can't help thinking Steven's observation about restless energy came from living with me, just as I know he was aware of his own personal dilemma:

I am thinking of the contemporary search for what might be called an honest open naturalness about life, an almost childlike acceptance of the facts of life in oneself and in others and nature generally. It is the quest for the freedom to be oneself, and to be freely and openly natural with others. . . .

And, as if he were speaking only about the two of us:

Also to be included is the use of psychotherapy and psychoanalysis as a way of honestly facing the facts about man's inner life, and a method of freeing men to be themselves.

(Later I had to laugh when I read in *New York* magazine that Abby Aldrich Rockefeller cited as the enemies of the Women's Liberation Movement "psychotherapy, psychology, and psychiatry . . . all of which reconcile women to the *status quo.*")

This was a very strong speech for the son of a leading Republican governor. Steven seemed to be more influenced by the Kennedys than by the Rockefellers. In truth, his speech did cause a lot of controversy, and his views on Vietnam caused more disagreement among the cousins than any other issue except Jay's becoming a Democrat.

The country was preparing for another national election. It was a time of acute tension in the nation, and Steven felt seriously involved in what was at stake, even before his father belatedly entered the Republican primaries and Robert Kennedy announced his candidacy for the Democratic nomination.

One night, I had the honor of meeting Senator Robert Kennedy at a small private gathering in New York to which Steven and I had been invited.

"Senator Kennedy," I said, "I am going to vote as a citizen for the very first time. I came this evening to decide whether to register as a Republican or a Democrat."

Steven and the Senator exchanged smiles that seemed to say "She's just teasing."

Robert Kennedy proved to be a true charmer, though he seemed more like a good-natured college boy than the mature and serious man suggested by the policies he espoused.

As the party ended and he was about to leave, the Senator, with his big and pleasing grin, whispered in my ear, "I hope you were able to make up your mind tonight."

Our social life was increasing by leaps and bounds. One day I was invited to attend a small private function, in the Governor's apartment, at which King Olav V of Norway was going to be the guest of honor. I began to have nightmares and the kind of jitters I hadn't felt since the early days of my marriage. I was once again an insecure island girl, with the polish and experience I had managed to gain over the past years erased by the words "King of Norway." I even went to the Norwegian Ambassador for some advice. He and his wife seemed perplexed and surprised by my anxieties, but they answered my questions about protocol with great care, kindness, and tact.

When I arrived at the Governor's apartment, I could see that my fears had been unfounded. As it turned out, there were many other Norwegians there, and, strangely, it was my countrymen who made me feel uncomfortable, not the King. None of them, however, made a particularly strong impression on me, and I am sure I had a similar effect on them. I definitely was not myself that day, and the only thing that made me smile was hearing the King laugh—which he did often and loudly. I looked at the Governor once or twice to see if the King's laughter upset him the way mine had when I worked for him.

Next day in the newspapers there appeared a large picture of the Governor, Happy, the King, and me on the balcony of the apartment. I was wearing my Sørlands *bunad*, the costume of southern Norway. One of the newspapers made a mistake and said I was the King's daughter instead of the Governor's daughter-in-law.

Steven and I were also invited to attend a dinner party in honor of Crown Prince Harald of Norway, at the residence of the Norwegian Ambassador. I was pleased to have the opportunity to meet the Crown Prince once again after my dismal first encounter, and grateful for the opportunity to rectify at least one bad impression on the Norwegian Royal Family.

I spent the whole day before the party trying to beautify myself. I knew that if I felt sure of my appearance I would have provided myself with at least a modicum of security.

Teasingly Steven asked, "How much do you think the Crown Prince will notice all of your preparations? Are you planning to show him your painted toenails?"

When we arrived at the official residence and met Crown Prince Harald again, he looked as though it had taken *him* only five minutes to dress for the party. His face was tan and healthy-looking, but his black suit appeared almost shiny with age. (We were told that he had been in a regatta that day and had made Norway look like a land of exceptional sailors.) The dinner conversations were long and not particularly interesting. After the meal, we all went to see a

Broadway play, and I sat next to the Crown Prince. He seemed as strained as the rest of the group, trying to enjoy the play and pretending to have a "marvelous time."

After the performance, the party proceeded to Delmonico's Hotel where we sat around a tiny table and a band played loud music. The walls were decorated with Egyptian pharaohs, and Steven kept trying to find a symbolic meaning in this. I was just trying to have a good time. Crown Prince Harald asked me to dance. I discovered that I felt very comfortable with him, and soon I was unreservedly telling him that when I was a little girl I had dreamed of living happily ever after with him in his castle. I quickly added that when I came to America my dream changed to one about being with Steven the rest of my life. I said to the Crown Prince, "I guess many girls dreamed of being in a castle with you." "Only special girls like you dreamed that," he said, and I thought he was comparing me to his beloved Sonja, who was also a commoner.

The next morning I received a telephone call from the Ambassador's wife telling me how much His Royal Highness had enjoyed his evening with the young people. Of course I was delighted, but as I placed my evening clothes to air by my dressing-room window, I did wonder about the evening. I thought of Steven up in his study, and I wondered if he felt Sonja was suited for the Crown Prince.

At an informal discussion that Steven and I were invited to, this time at the "Big House," I sat next to Dr. Henry Kissinger, of Harvard University, on a loveseat. Steven had told me he was a brilliant man who was giving his father political advice. I can remember trying to concentrate on the discussion, but Dr. Kissinger had a number of personal mannerisms that I found distracting. What comes back to me now is my effort to pay close attention, and not one single brilliant remark by him or by anybody else.

By the summer of 1968, the Governor's campaign for the

presidential nomination was in full, though belated, swing. I had no intention of becoming personally involved in his efforts until a friend, the wife of a Westchester psychiatrist, called me in excitement one day. She alluded to a "most fantastic idea," which she couldn't discuss over the telephone, and although I was suspicious of such secretive enthusiasm, I was also curious enough to invite her to Tarrytown.

My friend was an avid Rockefeller supporter who believed I could make a real contribution to the Governor's campaign. Thorough research had revealed that there were as many people of Norwegian background in Brooklyn alone as there were in all of Norway. She told me that never before in a presidential campaign had anyone ever tried to unite or solicit support from the Scandinavians as a voting bloc.

"With your love of Norway, your enthusiasm as a citizen of the United States, and your support for the Governor, you would be a natural to go out on the campaign trail to stalk the Scandinavian vote for your father-in-law."

I called the Governor to see what he thought of forming an organization to actively seek support from an ethnic group. When I told him that there were more than twelve million Americans of Scandinavian descent in the United States, and that they constituted an influential group politically, he became tremendously enthusiastic. He was further impressed by my offer to be a "Rockefeller for Rockefeller," and laughed when I said, "If the Kennedys can do it, so can the Rockefellers."

My first order of business was to find a place in which to carry out the ambitious undertaking. My friend and I spent one whole evening with a real-estate agent looking for a suitable headquarters. We seemed to be two aggressive women as we tried to secure a contract, immediately, for an architectural club off Park Avenue. Actually we were just big talkers who knew a bargain when we saw one. The building was scheduled to be demolished in the late fall, just after the elections, so the contract was really tailor-made for our purposes.

Soon I was busy decorating the headquarters, and the excitement and adrenalin surging through my body made me heady. I secured flags from the five Scandinavian missions after I promised that they would be properly hung or displayed. Within a short span of time the building was made ready, and a staff of eager volunteers was assembled. It was time to cut the ribbon for the official opening. The affair was well covered by the news media.

We asked L. J. Sverdrup, a retired Major General of the United States Army, to be chairman of the board of Scandinavians for Rockefeller, and I was appointed the national chairman. A poster was specifically designed for us, and we were on our way. We spent hours trying to elicit from a few influential Scandinavian-Americans the names and political persuasions of others in the United States. I began to make personal phone calls and written appeals for donations, and although I found it difficult at first being Mrs. Steven Rockefeller and begging for funds, my enthusiasm soon outweighed my hesitancy.

Steven helped me preside over a party for Scandinavians at the Playhouse, which we believed should get the new organization off to a flying start with publicity and a maximum amount of Scandinavian good will. In order to make the event really spectacular, we rented a baby elephant who cost four hundred dollars and was called Daffodil. Approximately two hundred and fifty guests came to the estate to enjoy Scandinavian food and music and the Indian elephant. I apologized for this far-from-Scandinavian import, with her sign that read SWING WITH ROCKY, but the reporters and photographers loved her.

In order to add a little color to the New York political scene, we held a "Luv the Guv" party at the Cheetah

Discotheque, in co-operation with the "New Majority" and "People for Rockefeller." A song, "Join Hands for Rockefeller," was introduced and well received. Steven's two sisters, Ann and Mary, were there to lend support. I had spent a great amount of time trying to make myself look attractive for the occasion and felt I was rather well turned-out. Perhaps I looked too self-satisfied, because Ann asked me, "Are you campaigning for Father or for yourself?"

In my search for something to add zest to the campaign, I got in touch with Pete Seeger. I thought he could possibly aid us as sort of a coalition entertainer for the "People for Rockefeller" and the "New Majority." He responded to my inquiry promptly and graciously. He was an earnest man, with a cause of his own, and he told me quite honestly that he could not personally and publicly endorse any of the candidates, because of his own political position in the country at the time. Although he didn't mention it, I was aware that he had disagreed with my father-in-law on an environmental issue connected with a proposed highway along the Hudson. Mr. Seeger began telling Steven and me about a project of his own that he believed might save the Hudson River. He explained that he had a ninety-foot sloop called *Clearwater*, which he hoped would sail the Hudson under the sponsorship of the Scenic Hudson Preservation Society, reminding people wherever it stopped that the river was polluted and that it was up to each individual to help make it clean again. Mr. Seeger planned to give free concerts at night wherever the sloop was moored.

Both Steven and I became almost as interested in *Clearwater* as we were in his father's bid for the presidency. We told Mr. Seeger that somehow, between bouts of campaigning, we would sandwich in a fund-raising party for him, too.

I decided the barn on the family farm would be an ideal place for a large gathering. Mr. Seeger brought along a young singer named Don MacLean, and the evening was a delightful mixture of guitar playing, singing, and foot tapping, though the opportunity for a little fund raising wasn't overlooked by Mr. Seeger and his entourage. After the party, a small group of us went back to our home. Don MacLean sang again there, in his especially gifted way, and Steven prophetically told him that he would go far with his clear voice and the sincere messages his songs carried.

After the party, Mr. Seeger sent a thoughtful letter commending Steven and me for being "searching and honest people in today's wealthy America," and invited us to become members of the Preservation Society in either a directorial or an advisory capacity.

"The Sloop Project," he wrote, "is but a step in the right direction. There is always the danger that we'll think one step is enough. But we also know the biggest task starts with one step."

From then on, my time was almost completely taken up by the campaign. After we had laid the groundwork for support on the local scene, plans were made for me to travel to the heavily Scandinavian areas in Pennsylvania, Minnesota, Iowa, Wisconsin, and many other places.

When little Stevie was told about my projected travels he said, "Oh, Mommy, do you have to go?" I told him that I was going to work hard for his grandfather. "You'll have to look hard to find a better man than Grandaddy, Mommy," he said, and from then on his prayers were amended with the plea, "and please make Granddaddy President of the United States."

Soon I was on my way, on a barnstorming schedule that was jam-packed with meetings, TV appearances, visits to old people's homes, Head Start centers, and correctional schools for teen-agers. Such places were not strongholds of the voting population, I knew, but these people were often neglected in the crush of the usual campaign.

The spontaneous way in which I answered questions or volunteered personal feelings during the campaign was described by reporters as "natural charm." The inner doubts and the lack of confidence I exhibited on several occasions were viewed as "dignity and reserve."

Every place I went it was reported that Cinderella had come to campaign for Rockefeller. During the whole tour, I made no formal speeches or major addresses, preferring instead to stick to my informal way with reporters and party members. Whenever I had to attend a large dinner, I made only perfunctory remarks from the dais, and then went around afterward to speak to people at their individual tables.

My method of campaigning was labeled "soft sell, " but it was the style I knew best, and it proved to be effective. I was really out of my element whenever any serious questions of policy came up, and played it safe by saying "The Governor can speak for himself on that matter."

I continued to win votes for Mr. Rockefeller in the best way I knew how, really the only way—by talking about myself, Steven, the children, the Rockefeller family, and hobbies—preferring to leave Vietnam, civil rights, and other American problems to the rest of the Rockefellers, who had spent whole lifetimes studying such matters.

In one of my interviews, which was dotted with "As I said to Steven" or "Steven thinks," the reporter concluded: "It is obvious that this fairy-tale romance is proving to be a happy one."

It seemed strange to me to still have so many Americans interested and intrigued by my "romantic marriage," even in the midst of a presidential election: "Mrs. Rockefeller, how did you meet your husband?"

"I thought the whole world knew that."

"Mrs. Rockefeller, what is it really like to be married to a Rockefeller?"

"I have the same desires and interests as most every other married woman. My main interest is wanting a good home and a happy family life. It's very important. No matter what other accomplishments one may have, if you don't have a good home then you don't really have anything."

About three-quarters of the way through the trip, the schedule and the pace started to become grueling. I don't think I had worked so hard physically in a long time, and I began to feel the effects of the generally easy life I'd led since my marriage. No matter how tired I got, though, I kept up my strenuous schedule, usually beginning every day with a visit from the local hairdresser at 6 A.M. in order to be presentable for my countless pictures with children, dogs, and Scandinavian flags.

Toward the end of the trip, we made a stop at the home of Frank Lloyd Wright. When I arrived at the airport, I remarked, "I think there are more Norwegians here to greet me than in the whole country back home."

Later, I told Iovanna, Frank Lloyd Wright's daughter, about Steven's preoccupation with designing our home, and she knowingly nodded her head. Because of our interest in Mr. Wright's work, Mr. Sam Johnson, of the Johnson Wax Company, gave us a tour of its beautiful Racine, Wisconsin, building, which had been designed by Mr. Wright. During the tour, somebody mentioned that there were one hundred Rasmussens listed in the Racine phone book, and I remarked, "And they are probably all my relatives at the moment."

Finally the trip was over. The press had treated me exceptionally well, the constituents had responded warmly, and I was beginning to feel that I was truly becoming "someone in my own right."

After I arrived home I began to notice that people were beginning to notice me, and to say that *Steven* was the lucky one. Once I overheard somebody say to him "You are a lucky

man to be a Rockefeller and to have Anne-Marie." Maybe his
sister Ann did have a point about *my* campaign.

After my expenditure of energy on behalf of his father,
Steven admitted that the lure of politics was drawing him
more and more into the center of the campaign, but he
described himself as a "behind-the-scenes idea man." When
people asked him about his father's chances in Miami, he
would say, "He wants the presidency. He believes he can do
it. So I say more power to him. Anne-Marie and I are doing
what we can to help him."

Steven did emerge from behind the scenes, and he mostly
discussed issues. One day the two of us were interviewed by
a reporter, and among other things Steven said, "I would
like to see Father listen to the voice of my generation. As a
father he has always been an open-minded man. . . . He
gave all of us an education you couldn't get from school or
from TV—a consciousness of what is going on. . . . The
intellectual world reflects the political and social world.
And there's the same confusion because there isn't one man
to listen to—anyone to whom one can look for guid-
ance. . . . Martin Luther King, Jr., will go down as the
Jeremiah of our times. He lived the relation between religion
and politics. The meaning of his life as the important event
in the religious life of the West will continue to grow. He
lived and acted what for the the rest of us is mostly a matter
of theory."

I thought Steven's remarks sounded like a nomination
speech for Martin Luther King instead of his father, but
when I was asked to comment on them, I said, "I completely
agree. Steven is a marvelous teacher, you know."

Soon all the campaigning was over, and Steven and I
retreated to Maine for a long Labor Day weekend with the
children before we went to Miami.

The results of that disastrous convention are well known.

The conservative Republican delegates chose Mr. Nixon over the liberal, divorced Governor Rockefeller. There were thoughts, and perhaps hopes, that the Governor would leave the party that had rejected him and join a coalition party. He didn't.

When he finally addressed the convention, the delegates were less than thoughtful or accepting. They seemed to feel he had gotten his just reward, and that everything he stood for had been soundly rejected. At the time, I believed that rejection stemmed more from the delegates' distaste for his divorce and remarriage than it did from his ideological and personal differences with Mr. Nixon. To me, as to Steven, the Governor's policies at the time seemed to be just what the country needed. But in fact the tide was running strongly against any form of liberalism, as we all know now, so his politics as well as his private life worked against him.

Governor Rockefeller always had that dream about the presidency. I often thought the dream may have been more pleasing to him than the reality would have been, and I surmised that he might have deliberately, if unconsciously, sabotaged his own chances of fulfilling that dream. Perhaps I am too willing to accept my own theory about his failure to achieve the presidency because of my own tendency to find dreaming more exciting and worthwhile than actuality. But I still believe that, to recognize this destructive tendency, one has only to look at how close he was to achieving his goal when, against everyone's advice, he married Margaretta Murphy.

When I saw Mr. Rockefeller "lose" in Miami, his face seemed relieved and I detected a sort of inner release. There were no battle scars, no lamenting, no sour grapes. The Governor was called a "good loser," especially in comparison with Richard Nixon. I disagree. I don't think he ever really wanted to win in the first place, so he played his losing cards right, and not from underneath the table, either.

The only sad faces after the convention belonged to those few supporters who had already imagined themselves settled in Washington, giving advice to the "Chief." (There was a joke that Dr. Kissinger was Mr. Rockefeller's congratulatory gift to Mr. Nixon after the convention.) Mr. Rockefeller's real followers looked forward to another four years of "dreams," as New York's "Chiefy" pointed at least New York State, if not the country, in the right direction.

He was very appreciative of his loyal supporters, as expressed in a letter to me shortly after the convention:

Albany
August 28, 1968

Dear Mia:

You never cease to amaze me! You did a superb job putting together Scandinavians for Rockefeller, and if I had had you working on all the ethnic and other groups, the result in Miami Beach would have been entirely different.

Congratulations on the wonderful group of people you assembled in remarkably short time, on my behalf. I really think you are out of this world, and I know Happy and I are fortunate to have you firmly in the family circle.

Thanks so very much.

With affectionate regard,

Sincerely,
Nelson

Nelson Rockefeller wasn't the only loser in the campaign. Whatever brief periods of happiness and peace Steven and I had enjoyed as a couple seemed to fade away entirely when the excitement and social whirl that had enveloped me this past year came to an end. Those moments were buried under the larger measurements of time—the weeks and months and years that we had been steadily growing apart. The story-book romance and the fairy-tale marriage had turned into a tragic saga, read by many and understood by too few. The central characters had lost the main thread of the story in order to find escape routes of their own—each driven by a need for survival as an individual rather than as a partner to a marriage.

Fortunately for all of us, we were able to go on fulfilling our roles as parents. The love and attention the children received from both of us provided them with a steady, stable, and realistic idea of what life is all about. They seemed to receive and respond well to the two types of attention and affection we gave them, and this enabled them to become what we individually were not—natural, spontaneous, bright—without making sacrifices for one another. They also were and remain able to give affection and love. Steven once demanded, "How can you give something you never really had enough of?" But our children will not be hampered that way.

Indeed, they did experience love—from both of us. They laugh and cry and are not afflicted with a societally imposed façade. How, having failed each other so miserably, we were so conscientious regarding the children, I shall never know.

Just at the time when our marriage was desperately straining at the seams, we were invited by Pete Seeger to attend a *Clearwater* sloop party in Bristol, Maine, to baptize the boat on behalf of Nelson A. Rockefeller, Governor of New York. We decided to go because both of us continued to hold him in high esteem, and we were still as concerned as he was about the future of the Hudson River.

When it came time to leave, I awaited Steven at the airport until it was dangerously close to departure time. Our suitcases were already aboard the plane. It got later and later. I became angry. Another intellectual lapse, I thought; he was probably so busy with his nose in a book that he had forgotten all about space and time, as he frequently did. Then I became concerned. I decided to let the plane and our luggage leave without me, for fear something had happened to Steven.

When he finally arrived on the scene, long after the plane had taken off, he was contrite and apologetic. He told me we wouldn't miss the affair, because he would drive us there. We spent almost the whole trip in the silence that had become habitual between us. Late that night we stopped at a small motel, where we felt funny admitting that it was late, that we had no luggage, and that our name was Rockefeller.

I took a bath and wrapped myself in a sheet. On the television set in our room a black man was singing "What the World Needs Now Is Love, Sweet Love."

I broke the silence: "You know, Steven, I have to agree with him."

We both laughed then, and it was the first laughter we had shared in a long time. I wished we could have started our honeymoon at that moment. Somehow it finally didn't matter that we were in a motel room not exactly recommended by Duncan Hines, neither one of us with any expectations or illusions. What counted was that, right then, we were just enjoying each other's comfort and love.

Next morning Steven had to wake early to drive out to the airport to retrieve our luggage. When we arrived at the dock where *Clearwater* was anchored, Steven and I shared his picnic lunch, mine having been eaten by a stray black dog. We listened to Pete Seeger and the Reverend Kirkpatrick sing catchy tunes about pollution, politics, and people. At one point Mr. Kirkpatrick remarked good naturedly, "We used to sing down in Louisiana about getting shoes on the other side. But let me tell you, Mr. Rockefeller, I'd rather have my shoes on this side if you don't mind." This impressed Steven so much that he has contributed annually to the Many Races Cultural Foundation, of which Reverend Kirkpatrick is the founder and remains the director.

A photographer appeared and took our picture. He observed that we looked as happy as newlyweds. In truth, it was probably the happiest weekend we'd had as man and wife.

That was in May. In June 1969, I left for Norway. Steven planned to stay home in his cabin and work on his doctoral dissertation. Possibly he would join us in August.

I had thought of Norway as a constant, where nothing ever seemed to change; and when I arrived I tried to feel and act as though I had never left home. But this time I was too restless. So many changes had taken place within me this past year—and, after all, things had changed in Norway, too.

Pappa was dreadfully sick, not quite bedridden but almost incapacitated. He loved having the children and me around him, but even though he was so ill, I couldn't stay home every day like the dutiful daughter I should have been, sitting at his side, talking about island days and Steven and the children while we drank coffee and ate cake. Instead, I stayed at Ormelia, and traveled around Norway as well. I was not at peace with the world at all.

I invited Mary Strawbridge and two other American friends to come to Norway to visit me. Mary arrived first, and then my friend Betty. Another friend, Jennifer Saltonstall, who had lived in the same apartment building as Steven and I when we were first married, and after whom our daughter Jennifer is named, planned to join us in Denmark.

Mary, Betty, and I had a good although exhausting time in Kristiansand and Oslo. Then Mary returned home, and Betty and I proceeded to Denmark, where we met Jennifer. She had been divorced and was taking this trip in order to provide herself with some "space" before entering into her second marriage. I think all three of us were experiencing marital problems and insecurities at the time, but we managed to avoid searching discussions about our personal situations.

Outdoors at Pocantico Hills, winter 1969
© Dan Budnik

The two girls and
sculpture by Henry Moo

Father and son on Steven's hill, 1968

Ras-Rock from the back lawn

In Norwegian costume

Three of
Anne-Marie's
flower
arrangements

Philippe Pouliopoulus

Anne-Marie on the terrace at Ras-Rock, 1974

Perhaps it was because we three shared general doubts about ourselves then—or more probably it was because I was a good persuader—that we decided to forgo the sight-seeing, the guidebooks, and the museums and castles, in order to do some mountain climbing. Back to Norway we went to pick up my blue Mustang, which I had brought along from the United States. Soon we were inside the car, setting off like so many Edmund Hillarys in search of a mountain to conquer. Neither of my friends had ever done any mountain climbing before—in fact, I don't think Jennifer had ever even climbed subway steps in New York—so we had to stop and buy all sorts of new and expensive gear for them. Then we set forth again, making for Galdhøpiggen, which, at 2,469 meters, is the highest mountain north of the Alps. For practice we decided to try a small mountain called Bittihorn, in the valley of Jotunheim, in the middle of Norway, reputed to be a pleasant afternoon's walk. But it cost us six exhausting hours and a number of blisters to reach the top of that relative molehill, so I had my doubts as I asked the proprietor of a charming tourist hotel about our chances of success at climbing Galdhøpiggen. He said that if we had a sunny day we'd surely reach the top—though of course we'd have to use pickaxes and ropes, an array of which he proceeded to show us.

More dubious than ever, Betty went to sleep at ten o'clock saying "Count me out." And I suspect all three of us were praying for a rainy, foggy day that would give us an excuse for not attempting the *real* mountain.

But next morning was undeniably clear and still, so, after breakfast, we set out to meet our young guides at the foot of Galdhøpiggen. We discovered that we had to pay a toll, but none of us had a cent; our guides obligingly lent us the money. Jennifer's feet had been bandaged because of the Bittihorn climb, and Betty seemed too small to hold the pack on her back. The guides took that from her and looked at us in disbelief. I guess they knew they would earn their pay on this trip.

To ensure our safety as we approached the glacier that has to be traversed a short way below the summit, the guides tied ropes around our waists, linking us to one another. By the time the summit came into view, Jennifer and I were badly out of breath, but Betty—who hadn't had to carry that pack—seemed as fresh and nimble as ever. The guides released her from the rope, and she seemed almost to fly up the last ascent, and reached the top ahead of everybody else. After we joined her, the guides gave her back the pack, and one of them asked, "American? American Indian?"

The three of us kept looking at each other in amazement. But despite the farcical episodes, something special happened to us emotionally and physically on that climb. As we all stood at the summit, looking out at the tremendous view, I was very proud—of myself, of Norway, and of my two American friends.

Betty kept singing "What goes up must come down," but the coming down wasn't difficult at all. It was as if the successful climb had restored our breath as well as our faith in ourselves. I couldn't wait to get back to the hotel so I could wire Steven about our adventure.

The next day, after a long sauna and a good night's sleep, we set off for Kristiansand S. We all felt ready to go home now, and, back in Søgne, my friends made plans to return to the United States together, and I settled down again with Mamma, Pappa, Torhild, and my children.

Steven sent me a generally chatty letter, complimenting us on our climb and telling me that he had turned in his 206-page philosophy paper. He also described his Fourth of July weekend with his sister Ann. Proudly he wrote:

> *Tarrytown*
> *July 29, 1969*
> *I finally finished the walk to the main door of my cabin. This*

morning a big buck looked in at me. It's a beautiful retreat, and I
am happy with it, but I do miss you, the children, and the joy of
working regularly with people. I hope my intellectual life and the
seclusion it has involved will soon lead to a more social life once
again. When I come, remember I love kids and teen-agers—fill the
house with them for me. The only thing I am leary of is endless
coffee parties with the adults.

Give my love to Steven, Ingrid, and Jennifer. Tell Stevie that his
sunflowers are bigger than he is. Tell Ingrid her flowers are coming
out and they are beautiful. Tell Jennifer her carrots and turnips are
delicious! Give them all big hugs and kisses.

He-She and Nissen are fine, but big nuisances. He-She still does
her business all over the house, and Nissen got Uncle Laurance out
of bed the other night by barking at his house. . . .

Much love to you, Mia.

XOX

Be patient with my letter writing. Love to Kristian and Lovise . . .

Granted Steven didn't write often, but what a comforting
and happy letter when he got around to it!

Two weeks later, my world crashed. August 1, 1969.

Pappa was dead!

One of the last things he said to me before he closed his
eyes was, "I understand you, Mia, and I love you."

The very next day I received a thick-looking letter from
Steven. How relieved I was at first to think I was hearing
from him when I desperately needed to.

The letter began with "PLEASE READ IN QUIET AND PRIVATE
PLACE."

He started off by telling me about all the rain in Tarrytown.
He then said that since I had left he had spent all his time
thinking, thinking, thinking. Gradually, during the quiet of
these days, he had been reflecting on all that had happened
to us over the years and this past winter. There had been
bright moments, yes, but we had not ever really been happy
together for any length of time. He did not blame anyone, he
wrote. It was just a fact.

He told me that in view of his feelings he could not think

of coming to Norway to see my family and to celebrate an approaching anniversary party. He said he would like to see Kristian one more time, but under the circumstances he felt his visit would be hypocritical and a sham. He also thought that people would probably see through our little role-playing as the happy couple.

Sometime during the spring of that year, when I was feeling desperate, I had reached the point of suggesting that we get divorced. In this letter, Steven reminded me that he hadn't been able to accept that suggestion. He had stubbornly clung to his ideal of working out our marriage. But the problem was that we had tried—so hard, so long—and still there was a great gulf between us. Neither of us had been able to love the other in a way that was satisfactory to the other. Could we in the future? he asked. What had troubled him so much this summer was that he had begun to have serious doubts that we could. Now that summer was coming to an end. I was in Norway. He was in Pocantico. Both in our own separate worlds. Did he really look forward to coming to Norway? He certainly missed the children very much, he said, and he did not like being apart from them all summer. And although he would like to see my father one more time, he was very dissatisfied with our relationship. He felt more than ever the strain under which we had been living, and the deep personal need to experience something better. He hardly felt ready to take me on a relaxed four- or five-day trip to Copenhagen or the mountains. His heart simply would not be in it. . . .

Where did this all lead us? He did not yet know. We would certainly have to talk it over quietly somewhere, and make every effort to protect the children from being any more upset than necessary. He said how much he hoped his letter was not too much of a shock for me, and he believed that in the past I had perhaps been more willing to see the truth of our relationship than he had. I had often suggested that maybe we were just not suited to each other, and maybe I had been right. . . .

He wrote without bitterness, he told me. He wanted to do what was best for me, for himself, and for the children. What other people thought was irrelevant now. Perhaps I would even find this letter a relief. I must not suspect from all this that he had found another person to take my place. He had not. He was living there just as he usually did. He was only thinking out loud or in writing. Deep down inside, he believed, I must feel about this problem much as he did. That was all he had to say. It was still raining, and he was still thinking.

"Love, Steve," he wrote at the end.

Pappa's death numbed the blow of that letter. I couldn't allow myself the luxury of self-pity or sadness. Real, deep, and honest grief was the first priority. I was in a state of shock over the loss of my father, and one doesn't really enter two states of shock simultaneously.

Steven did come to Norway to see "Kristian one more time" after all. He accompanied me to the funeral.

I stepped forward as Pappa's coffin was about to be carried out to the cemetery, and said: "It is with deep sorrow that I must put down this wreath on behalf of my sister and myself. We both loved you so very much, Pappa. Thank you for what you taught us about the seriousness of life. More important, thank you for how you lived your life. We have lost a good, kind, and understanding father. You will always be with us in spirit. I wish to put light and peace over your memory."

When I came back to stand next to Steven, he patted me gently on the back and said, "I am so sorry, Mia."

But apparently he had meant every word of his letter. I could tell by his reserve and aloofness, and his lack of overt sympathy for me, but he had been genuinely fond of my father. His whole family had been, in fact, and I received warm words of condolence from Steven's father:

I have thought so often of your great loss. Your father was such a strong man, who had all the qualities that made the Vikings and your country such a great nation. It is so sad that he is gone, but so wonderful that you could be there with him during his last days. . . . I know that his greatest pride and joy in this life was you. I don't blame him for being proud of you—you're a wonderful person with a wonderful family and a great many friends who are thinking of you especially now, and sharing your sadness.

With lots of love to you all,

Nelson

Mrs. Rockefeller also sent me a very warm and touching letter:

Mia Darling

. . . I can imagine the pain that you are going through. It certainly was a good thing that you and the children were there this summer. It must have brought him happiness to have you around him these past few weeks. You will always be glad you were able to do this. Losing one's father is a very sad thing and leaves one with a real ache in the heart. . . . You can treasure memories of a wonderful father. He was truly a very dear and special man. Everyone who met him or knew him felt this. . . . It helps to know others share your loss. . . .

Somehow one always could communicate with him in a sort of human way. . . .

I am sure you have a great many problems to decide upon—one right after another. Dear Mia, I wish I were there right now to give you a big hug. If I can help by coming and taking the children, do let me know. . . .

From your affectionate mother-in-law,
Mary C. Rockefeller

I did have a great many problems to decide upon, one right after the other; and I couldn't bring myself to add to Mamma's burden by discussing my personal problems with her at that time. I had to get home to Tarrytown as soon as it was feasible, to sort things out in my mind and heart, and with Steven. More than a small feeling of resentment began to develop within me. How dare he leave now, just when I felt some headway had been made with our problems? I was just beginning, for the first time in my life, to face things as they were and not as I imagined or wanted them to be. I was just on the verge of becoming someone in my own right. I was making the transition from thinking of myself as the luckiest maid in the world to being a woman who felt she had something to contribute to her husband and children and to life in general. I went through all sorts of recriminations about myself and about Steven. I thought of the careful bird watcher, the patient man, the thoughtful man; I wondered how his patience, love, and years of study could permit him to abandon hope—especially now, when I was no longer his island girl, his sweet and natural *hausfrau*. As soon as I spoke these thoughts out loud, I knew this was the reason for the "Why now?"

Knowing what I had to face when I returned to Tarrytown, I asked my sister to come and stay with me for a while.

After I reached home, my melancholy increased. As we began to discuss our plans for the termination of our marriage, it became overwhelming..

Steven and I had gone to see Dr. Weber together before I went to Norway. In the course of that meeting I had run out of the office twice because I was so upset. Dr. Weber had said to me: "Steven loves you as much as he could love anyone. If it's not enough for you, you both should do something about it."

Now, as my depression deepened, I went into the city for another visit to Dr. Weber. (I was to see him many times in the next eight or nine months, and he really upheld me during that difficult period.) I made plans to spend the night with Mrs. Rockefeller, who showed as much love, understanding, and warmth to me as my real mother could have. I took my Chinese Shih-Tzu along for company. The next morning I awoke to discover that the little dog had gone out on Mrs. Rockefeller's terrace and fallen through the balustrade, and lay dead on the pavement below. I got into my car and drove directly to a place where I knew Shih-Tzus were bred, and bought another. I couldn't stand having a third void in my heart to fill.

The dear little puppy was a momentary diversion from my sadness, but as days piled one upon the other I thought I would lose my mind. Nothing definite was happening yet: there were only *plans* for separation. Tension was all around me. One day I was slicing some lemons for tea with Mrs. Rockefeller, and she observed that I was cutting them too thick. I got so angry at what I thought was her frugality that I took the whole lemon and threw it at the sink. We both felt sorry immediately, and I could see that Mrs. Rockefeller, too, in her own way, was disturbed and upset about our situation. I truly felt her love and support.

I spent a great many hours during that period simply retreating to my dressing room, pulling down my shades to keep out the sun, yet not enough to block the view of the Hudson. I stared at that unchanging, majestic river for more hours than I care to remember.

One day a painter from Scarborough, Dick Hurd, requested that he be allowed to paint my portrait. Why not? It would give me an excuse to sit and stare in my dressing room. Steven thought it was a bit presumptuous at my age. He told me people usually don't sit for portraits until after they have done something significant with their lives. My mind went to the formal portraits of the Rockefeller family that preside over the large room in the Playhouse, but I didn't care. I thought if I didn't have my likeness captured now there might not, at a later date, be anything left of me to paint.

Mr. Hurd came and began the arduous task. Many days he brought recordings of lively music with him, in order to evoke some sign of animation in my eyes. When he eventually finished, I took one look at the haunted face he had captured and at the slightly slumped posture that could have been used for a textbook illustration of brooding melancholia and I wept for the reality of my situation.

On October 9, 1969, Steven moved into his cabin. The same night I sat down and wrote two letters. The first was to Mamma:

Tarrytown
October 9, 1969

Dear Mamma,

This is surely one of the most difficult letters I have ever had to write to you.

It looks like the children and I will be living alone here on the estate by the middle of October. At this point it seems best that Steven and I not live together any more in order to avoid hurting each other.

It is not a question of which of us is right or wrong. We have both tried in our own ways to make sense of our marriage. Each of us has been lonely and unhappy.

I know you appreciate Steven—so do I, and will continue to do so.

I beg you, Mamma, not to judge, especially before you see all the pieces of the puzzle in the right place. There have been many things about which you were never told. I promise, I have tried.

I can only wish now to be a good mother to the children and to try to find meaning in my life without Steven. I am finally realistic enough to know there is no hope for reconciliation. Please do not write any accusatory words either to Steven or to me.

I am grateful to you for allowing Torhild to come to be with me at this time. She has been able to see the situation from both sides. Perhaps you could come to me when Torhild goes home. I need your love and understanding now more than ever in my life. Perhaps after Pappa's death we both need each other now—we seem to have deeper feelings and more sympathy for each other.

Please do not be sentimental or sad.

Also do not worry about finances or have any anxieties in that area, for I will be able to help you for as long as I live.

As far as I know, the Rockefeller family remains fond of me and seems to understand what the situation is. Although Steven and I will not live together, we will remain close in a certain way. Neither doctors nor lawyers can erase a certain bond of a shared life.

When I am at rock bottom I will always think of you and Pappa and the strength you showed when he was ill and finally passed away. In the days to come, I hope you will be proud of me, too, even though there have been so many things that I have done to cause you sorrow. But I know that no one is more aware of the fact that deep down inside of me there is a will and a wish to improve and be good.

Please answer quickly as to whether or not you can come—you are much needed.

In ending this letter I must tell you, and this is no criticism of Steven, that if there must be one who has given up the struggle, it cannot be I.

I am psychologically tired out. I ask for your understanding, Mamma—I hope you will give it to me.

Many greetings, hopeful expectations, and my love to you. I am sorry for the suffering this letter will bring to you.

Love, Mia

I also wrote this fragment of a letter to Steven, but never had the courage to give it to him:

Tarrytown
October 9, 1969

Dearest Steven,

Well, Steven, did you ever think that I might be losing a husband but gaining three children? At last I am needed and loved. For the past years I have felt neither in our home.

We certainly were two lonely figures who made a big mess of our lives by trying to achieve harmony together.

I finally am becoming quenched of the incredible thirst for your love that never seemed forthcoming. No longer will you find me begging for your affection. I had to get so low before I realized I could be so strong. Not yet, but perhaps someday I will be able to laugh and look at the world with untired eyes.

I will always like you, Steven, but someday I will be free of loving you—for me that love has been like a disease.

You are intelligent and rich, but still poor. You might be surprised to find you need me, or someone like the "natural" girl you married, to make you feel whole and to make you forget about your name.

As usual, you are right in your realistic assessment of our situation. I, too, am beginning to see it clearly.

Anne-Marie

Mamma responded quickly and in her special way to my letter:

Lohne
October 18, 1969

My Mia,

I received your letter yesterday when I came back from town. It is difficult to tell you how I feel because when feelings get strong, I would rather be silent.

However, I had a feeling that there were problems in your marriage, although you never said anything. I have prayed to God that this would not be the outcome of the difficulties. I still have faith in Him that His way will become known and things will work out. I feel with you, and I feel for Steven. I am especially sorry for the children. Try to forget yourself and live together, if possible, for the sake of the children and the promise that you gave to each other ten years ago.

We all experience good and bad days. We all have a bad side to our nature which makes us behave egotistically at times. When we learn to live more for others than for ourselves, then happiness comes. If we come in humility and trust to God, we will never be disappointed. I believe that God will help at a time when we ourselves are unable to. His thoughts and His ways are far higher than ours—I have clearly discovered this during the past summer.

I would like to come and see you, but I am unable to say how long I can stay. Be grateful that you have such an understanding sister. She knows you, appreciates you, wishes the best for you—as we all do.

Remember, Mia, dear, there is power in folded hands. I send heartfelt and warm greetings—to you, Steven, and the children,

From your Mother

The time of Steven's actual leave-taking soon approached. It was a sad period for both of us. He told me that no longer could I claim to be the naïve little island girl. I had so much now. He also hoped that I would continue my artistic endeavors.

"Mia, you would make a wonderful wife for some aggressive politician, businessman, or diplomat."

He said that the only thing that could really impress him now would be the manner in which I raised our children, and his remark has so influenced my life that some friends teasingly call me a professional mother.

After Steven went to take up residence in his cabin in the woods, all the members of the family agreed that I could and should stay in our home for as long as I wished.

Probably to make me feel still a part of the family, I was invited to have dinner with Steven's father, Happy, and other guests, including their close friend Mrs. Vincent Astor. Mr. Rockefeller toasted me that evening by saying "Anne-Marie has given more to the Rockefeller family than we have given to her."

Mrs. Astor turned to me and said, "What are you going to do with yourself now, Anne-Marie?"

"Live, Mrs. Astor, live."

I looked around at the walls and the gates and the whole beautiful Rockefeller estate on my way back to Steven's house that night, and knew that if I was going to live I would have to find someplace where I could be free of the constant reminders of who I was not any more.

Two prominent lawyers met and began to work at the complicated business of untangling a fairy tale. We had quite a lot of property to divide, and it was very painful to go through ten years' worth of accumulated possessions and say, this is mine and that is yours.

We had a few major disagreements, one of which was about our king-sized bed. For some reason Steven wanted it, but I did, too. Besides, I knew it wouldn't fit into his cabin. My sister, though, prevailed upon me to be reasonable, and when Mary Jane, my elderly beautification partner, heard about my plight, she arranged for me to have an antique four-poster of hers that had been in storage, complete with canopy and linens. After the ruffles and the canopy were starched and ironed and the whole bed was fresh and clean, I must admit I did feel more secure and less alone in it—although I used to plump up some pillows and place some books on Steven's side, so as not to feel completely deserted.

Unfortunately, the atmosphere around the house began to take on as much gloom as if I had been widowed. Even the plants suffered, and meals were something simply to be endured for the sake of the children and dogs. Sleep became a precious commodity.

For the sake of my sanity and the health of the children, I knew it was time to give up living at Pocantico. After looking around with a real-estate agent, I finally purchased a large home in a countryside of woods and meadows, not far from a charming village, and I moved there in February 1970. On the property there was a beautiful lake, which was a perfect haven for frogs, ducks, turtles, and hovering dragonflies. And the trees were magnificent—especially the three proud weeping willows by the lake. As soon as I saw them I thought of them as symbols of my three children, and I knew the house was meant to be ours.

I called the place Ras-Rock. It was idyllic, and I thought from the beginning how perfect it would have been if we had been wise enough to have chosen a place like it for ourselves when we were first married, one that we would have owned personally. We would have been autonomous and free, outside any walls, living on a lane where we would have had regular neighbors.

The children were elated with the new and real country

home, where they had access to all types of nature, pets, and friends, and where they all noted there were no gates or gatemen. It was a new but exhausting responsibility for me to be so close to my children and bring them up alone. In calling the property Ras-Rock, I intended to bring the best of both the worlds those names stood for into my new life, where I would not be living on an island or in an illusion.

Afterword

The children and I are still living at Ras-Rock, four years after my marriage to Steven Rockefeller ended, and two years after the end of a brief second marriage that has no place in this story. In many ways it is a quiet life, very different from my life with Steven, but it is a busy one, too, for all of us.

Young Steven, who for the last three years has been attending a day school for boys, is very serious about his studies, and he has been active in sports. Ingrid and Jennifer, like so many girls, love horseback riding and skiing and swimming, and they are also interested in modern dance. My own days are spent running a rather large house and supervising the care of the grounds, which mean more to me all the time. My shrubs and my trees, especially those three beautiful weeping willows, are like close and dear friends to me—with whom I never have any arguments! A great many animals come and go at Ras-Rock; besides our cats and dogs we have had ducks and ducklings, chameleons, fish, rabbits, and a horse that I kept at a nearby stable. (When my accountant raises her eyebrows over the vet's bills, I tell her they're better than bills from a psychoanalyst would be.) I take photographs endlessly, and I still find myself enthusiastically supporting various causes. I spend a good deal of time traveling—often alone, but sometimes with the children, while they are still young enough to enjoy going places with their mother.

The town I live in is small and beautiful, but it is a community for couples, where life would probably be very different, and where I think I would feel really at home, if Steven and I were still married. Now, instead of going out a lot myself, I prefer to entertain at home, partly so the children can meet a variety of people and feel at ease with adults outside their family. Very often our guests are young students from foreign countries, and the children enjoy being with them as much as I do. The girls take part in serving our guests. Always, in cold weather, we love to have an open fire, and Steven carries on his father's tradition by making sure it keeps going well through the evening.

I stay in close touch with Mamma and Torhild. Mamma, alone now, cares for her little home at Lohne, in Søgne, and visits her family and friends, driving around in the VW that is really her closest friend of all. She has come to stay with us many times, but she will always believe that Norway is a better and easier country to live in. Torhild works in a government office in Kristiansand S, as an assistant to the doctor who is in charge of specialized medicine in the southern part of Norway. She calls home daily to chat with Mamma, and she visits her every other weekend. She has never married.

As for Steven—I am finally, after all these years, beginning to accept the fact that I can live without him and not die inside. Sometimes I am even able to think of him almost as a stranger. But he is also a special and most important friend, with whom I have an unusually good understanding regarding our children. We are in constant touch and discuss whatever problems come up. We feel that this gives young Steven and Ingrid and Jennifer the security they need. It reminds them that their parents still have *them* in common—and that is perhaps the most important thing of all.

Steven is now a professor teaching at a small college in New England. The children visit him often—as they and I often visit Grandmother Rockefeller—and now that our son is really growing up, I try to arrange for him to spend as much time as possible with Steven. The two of them, for instance, recently visited various boarding schools together so that young Steven could decide which one he wanted to attend. He will be away from home, attending the school of his choice, by the time this book is published.

Sometimes it seems impossible that so many years have gone by since our son was born. Then, in a mirror, I see the gray in my hair, and I can believe that he will soon be a young man. I think I have in some ways said good-bye to Steven because of time, which keeps passing, and which in the end heals all wounds. One of my strongest wishes is to know that he is content in his private life—that, although he has yet to marry again, he does not feel crushed and lonely, as I often do.

I find that music helps. I play my many records more often during long quiet evenings, and tell myself that nobody needs to be really alone, for here are all these great musical talents, giving themselves freely for our enjoyment. And I try to see my life as my own, really *mine*—not what my family and friends think it should be. I certainly do not anticipate a perfect life any more. Each experience I have had has taught me a great deal about life—but also, much more important, about my own self. I think of what someone recently said to me: "It is not how many times you fall; it is how many times you are able to get up." So maybe, at last, I have become more of a realist. I wish to think so, at least.

But I know I'll always be romantic in some ways. I have a recurrent daydream about the wedding of one of our children, and about how I will dance just once more with Steven and say "Guggen" to him again, and after that be silent. By that time, I am certain, another Mrs. Steven C. Rockefeller will be waiting to dance with her husband. But the music does not stop. Love is all around. Yes, I am still romantic, but I am not going to let my feelings take over. I know that I have learned from my illusions.

This is how one love story can end.

March 1974

Index

INDEX